Strategy

*Churches Making
Disciples for the
Next Millennium*

2000

Other Books by Aubrey Malphurs

Biblical Manhood and Womanhood
Developing a Mission for Your Ministry
Developing a Vision for Ministry in the 21st Century
Maximizing Your Effectiveness
Planting Growing Churches for the 21st Century
Pouring New Wine into Old Wineskins
Values-Driven Leadership
Vision America: A Strategy for Reaching a Nation

Strategy 2000

Churches Making Disciples for the Next Millennium

Aubrey Malphurs

kregel
PUBLICATIONS

Grand Rapids, MI 49501

Strategy 2000: Churches Making Disciples for the Next Millennium

Copyright © 1996 by Aubrey Malphurs

Published by Kregel Publications, a division of Kregel Inc., P.O. Box 2607, Grand Rapids, MI 49501. Kregel Publications provides trusted, biblical publications for Christian growth and service. Your comments and suggestions are valued.

For more information about Kregel Publications, visit our web site at www.kregel.com.

Cover photo: Photodisc, vol. 4
Cover design: Alan G. Hartman
Book design: Nicholas G. Richardson

Library of Congress Cataloging-in-Publication Data
Malphurs, Aubrey.
    Strategy 2000: churches making disciples for the next millennium / Aubrey Malphurs.
        p.   cm.
    Includes bibliographical references and index.
    1. Discipling—Christianity I. Title.
BV4520.M35   1996   266'.001—dc20   96-30480
                                                                    CIP

ISBN 0-8254-3196-4

Printed in the United States of America
2 3 4 / 04 03 02 01 00 99 98

To my friends
Rick Warren, Bill Hull, and Bob Gilliam
who have catalyzed my thinking
in the areas of strategy and
disciplemaking.

Contents

Part 3: The Product of Developing a Strategy

Appendixes

Introduction

Faith Chapel Church is located at the hub of Garland, Texas, one of many suburbs bordering Dallas, Texas, on the east. Several young, visionary families bravely ventured out as pioneers in the 1930s to found Faith Chapel when Garland was merely an annoying series of stoplights and a gas station or two along one of the main arteries that led motorists from Dallas to east Texas. As Dallas grew and spilled over into Garland, the church grew with the community. In the 1950s, as the GIs from World War II began families, the church swelled in size, growing from a mere handful to around 350 young, robust families.

Today the church finds itself in what has become a different and somewhat decaying community. A quick tour of the immediate neighborhood reveals a number of dilapidated houses with an older-model Texas Cadillac (a pickup truck) parked squarely in an oil-soaked, weed-infested front yard. Most of those who live around Faith Chapel speak Spanish and some speak Vietnamese, but most do not attend church. The few who do attend a church attend a Catholic church near by. On a good Sunday, perhaps 120 people who no longer live in the area are present at Faith Chapel. They are the faithful who drive some distance to the church every Sunday. Many of those whose names are still on the church roll are attending other churches since they have relocated to the suburbs— or they have dropped out altogether.

While the declining community has changed drastically, the white, Gothic church with its steeple and cross affixed on top has changed little over the past sixty years of its existence. Perhaps the most notable change is the age of the people in attendance. In the 1930s they were all young, venturesome families full of energy and excitement as they anticipated what God was about to do. Today, as you pan from one side of the sanctuary to the other, you see many empty pews and some pews populated mostly with gray heads. Many are oblivious to the situation.

They are content with the circumstances and are enjoying growing old together. Others, who are futurists, however, worry. Regardless, the one thing they all have in common is that no one ever talks about the church's decline. It is comparable to a sullen storm cloud that ominously hangs over their heads, ready to break down upon and drown them at any moment, but in their denial, no one is even carrying an umbrella.

Had you attended Faith Chapel in the 1930s, left for fifty years, and then returned recently, you would discover that the program has not changed appreciably. They have always believed that it takes "three to thrive"—a service on Sunday morning and evening plus a Wednesday night prayer meeting. So a dwindling number of wonderful, older people attend the adult Sunday school class where a semi-knowledgeable teacher and his wife lecture the faithful from the Bible. Both were founders of the church and are proud of it. In class they often find themselves reminiscing about what life was like at the church back in the 1940s and the 1950s—the "good old days."

Next, at 11:00 A.M. they dutifully attend the morning preaching service. Some (mostly the women) take notes and nod approvingly, while the men stare out the windows, fidget and look at their watches, or snooze. During the football and hunting seasons, the adult men are conspicuously absent from the 11:00 A.M. service, much to the displeasure of the women and the pastor. Perhaps twenty or thirty of the faithful, elderly residents return Sunday evening to hear another hour-long sermon.

The church finishes the week with a Wednesday evening prayer meeting that five to ten of the most faithful attend. To encourage these stalwarts, the former pastor once said: "You can tell how many people love the church by those who attend on Sunday morning. You can tell how many love the pastor from those who attend Sunday evening. But you can tell who really loves the Lord by those who come to Wednesday night prayer meeting!"

Eight years ago Pastor Robert Smith graduated from seminary and with great excitement and anticipation became the pastor of Faith Chapel Church. He has seen some changes but not much is happening spiritually. If it was not for a few younger families, he would describe himself as the caretaker and chaplain of a rest home. Please do not misunderstand, he loves these people. But lately, he has begun asking: Is this all there is to Christianity? Is this what ministry is all about? Is this what he spent three years in seminary studying theology, Greek, and Hebrew preparing to do? He is discouraged. He desires to give his life to a significant cause that will outlive him. But the situation at Faith Chapel is not exactly what he had envisioned. He is at a point in his life where he is standing on the ministry ladder leaning against the church wall and wondering if his ladder is leaning against the wrong wall. Did he make a mistake in leaving his former profession as an engineer? Did he make a mistake in going to seminary? Perhaps he would have a greater impact for Christ if he returned to the marketplace or leaned his ministry ladder against the parachurch wall.

As strange as it may seem, Pastor Smith has never been discipled. He was saved in church, but no one ever discipled him there. He approached his pastor about spending some time together, but the man indicated that he was so busy in ministry (primarily hospital, home, and rest home visitation) that he simply did not have the time. And even if he had the time, he confessed that he was not sure he knew what to do—no one had ever discipled him either.

Then Smith went to seminary where his professors and others talked about and lectured on discipleship. Though he had a great set of notes, no one discipled him there. Several professors said that the job of the church is to make disciples, but no one taught him how to do it or presented a strategy for accomplishing this in the church. A visiting lecturer once suggested that if the job of the church is to make disciples according to Matthew 28:19, then perhaps the requirement for graduation from seminary should not be the grades given but the disciples made during seminary. This idea was not received very well, so nothing more was said.

Faith Chapel has no disciple-making strategy in place outside the Sunday school and the Sunday morning and evening sermons. And few of the people in his church would claim to be Christ's disciples. Should you ask, they would not even know what a disciple is. The seminary trained Pastor Smith to be an expository preacher. So he has attempted to use the pulpit along with his Bible-based sermons on Sunday morning as a means to disciple his people. However, he has run into a growing dilemma that pastors face all over America as well as in the Bible Belt—sporadic attendance. A survey in the local paper revealed that many in the community are interested in spiritual things, but that only 30 percent attend church every Sunday. How can he possibly disciple people who are present only one or two Sundays every month? Even his most faithful attendees are absent at least once a month. Some are businessmen who are on the road. And a number of his elderly parishioners are struggling with ill health. Then there are the football and hunting seasons. Others attend Faith Chapel and one or two other churches in the area. All of which serve to raise the question: Is this sufficient to fulfill Christ's Great Commission to make disciples and win the world to Christ?

—————

Churches like Faith Chapel are sprinkled all across America. The fact is that most churches do not have an adequate strategy to fulfill the Savior's command to make disciples. In *Today's Pastors*, George Barna writes that less than 3 percent of pastors have developed a ministry marketing plan (which is similar to a disciple-making strategy), and less than one-fourth have a clear, well-articulated notion of their target audience.[1] Yet how can a church obey Christ's command without this?

Every church needs a process for making disciples as well as a model of a disciple-making church. The "three to thrive" concept and all its trappings have proved inadequate throughout much of the twentieth century. The verdict has long been in. It is not producing disciples. My observation is that many if not most of the churches that God is blessing are making disciples, and what they are doing can serve as a model for other churches. But the problem is that most attention is focused on the product rather than the process. Churches mistakenly ape the product only to fail miserably. This book provides a model of what a disciple-making church might look like. But it is only one of potentially numerous good models.

Church models can be helpful. They give us an idea of how someone else has discipled people. They also serve to catalyze our thinking so that we do not have to reinvent the proverbial wheel, yet come up with something creative and unique to our situation. But the pastor that mimics another church's model risks failure. The reason is that most often the pastor, his people, and the community are unique. While the model is important, just as important is the process one goes through to arrive at that model. What is needed is a tailor-made process that any pastor can lead his church through that considers who he is, who his people are, and the part of the country where they live and minister. The purpose of this book is to provide such a process.

As a church planter, established church pastor, writer, church consultant, Christian futurist, and player-coach of future leaders, I have spent much time studying what many of the churches that God is blessing are doing. I not only have examined the product but have also asked: What process are they following to arrive at their product? What process do they all share whether it is or is not intentional? What factors must they consider? What steps have they taken? This book is the result of my discovery.

You should know that some of my sources are secular books as well as religious. You will be able to spot them in the footnotes. By "secular" I mean books that are not intentionally written from a Christian perspective. This is not to say, however, that what they say is not based on truth. I am convinced that all truth is God's truth. All the content of the Bible is true (2 Tim. 3:16), but not all truth is found in the Bible.[2] If it were, then the Bible would be a massive book, too long for anyone to read through in an entire lifetime much less one sitting. For example, scientists have discovered the truth that if you brush and floss your teeth regularly, you will have fewer cavities. I have not found this truth in my Bible, although it could be hidden away somewhere in the dietary laws of Leviticus! But I would prefer not to find it in my Bible. There are more important things already there that will take me a lifetime to discover and apply.

I like to refer to these secular sources as "my Jethros." In Exodus 18 Jethro, Moses' father-in-law, advises Moses not to attempt to counsel all Israel by himself (a million or more people—Exod. 12:37–38), or he will wear himself out. Instead, he is to separate the people into sections of tens, fifties, hundreds, and thousands. Next, he is to select men of integrity and allow them to help him in the process by taking the sections and handling the majority of the cases in their section. Only the most difficult cases would reach Moses, who ministered at the top of this structure. What is interesting is that Jethro may not have been a believer, yet his excellent counsel that foreshadows modern management structure probably rescued Moses from a potential physical and emotional breakdown. The same can be said of some of the secular books of non-Christians in the marketplace today. In my case, however, theological study has provided me with a grid through which to screen and evaluate knowledge whatever its source since it is often difficult to determine truth outside the Bible.

Whether you are in a parachurch or a church ministry, it is impossible for you to do what God wants you to do without a strategy! The process for developing a strategy in this book applies to parachurch ministries as well as churches regardless the size—small or large.

This book is about ministry planning and how to develop a strategy for making disciples. The other element in the work of ministry, which I will assume from the outset, is the spiritual dimension. At the very heart of any ministry is the work of the Holy Spirit and the entire spiritual dimension. If the leadership and the people are not men and women of

God with an authentic passion for Christ, the best strategic planning in the world will not help them. Without him, we can accomplish nothing (John 15:4–5). Lost people are attracted to our ministry when they observe our authentic love for one another (John 13:34–35) rather than our excellent visions and strategies, as important as they are. It is hoped that when they see us, they will know that we have been with Jesus.

The book consists of three major parts. The first is entitled "The Preparation for Developing a Strategy." It consists of four chapters that provide the broad foundation upon which every strategy is built. The first chapter establishes the need for a strategy, and the second stresses the importance of the same. These two chapters throw down the challenge that catalyzes the process. They also provide the stamina that the leadership team needs to play hard in the late innings of ministry. The third chapter defines what a strategy is. It serves to clarify precisely what we are talking about. The fourth chapter presents a brief but necessary biblical theology of strategy in response to the question: Is it biblical?

The second part is entitled "The Process of Developing a Strategy." It builds upon the foundation provided by the first four chapters and presents the actual four-step process that a leader takes the ministry through to arrive at a strategy that is tailor-made for the ministry organization. The fifth chapter presents step 1. It provides the specific, hands-on preparation for developing the strategy such as the time, cost, readiness, location, and leadership factors. The sixth chapter is step 2 and helps leaders to determine their ministry's target person. It asks the very important question: Who are we trying to reach? The seventh chapter is step 3 and helps to determine the particular program for the target group. It asks: What kind of church will it take to reach our target group? The eighth chapter is step 4. It instructs leaders how to design a strategic plan that will implement the program developed in chapter 7.

The third part is entitled "The Product of Developing a Strategy." The result of the process in chapters five through eight is a product. The last two chapters present several different model strategies as products that illustrate what the process can produce. They will catalyze leaders' creativity and give them some ideas of what they might develop. Chapter 9 presents a model disciple-making strategy for a new paradigm church for the twenty-first century.[3] Chapter 10 provides the reader with other model strategies that individual churches, denominations, and parachurch ministries have developed to fulfill Christ's Great Commission.

ENDNOTES

1. George Barna, *Today's Pastors* (Ventura, Calif.: Regal Books, 1993), p. 105.

2. See my discussion of this concept in *Maximizing Your Effectiveness* (Grand Rapids, Mich.: Baker Book House, 1995), pp. 62–64.

3. New paradigm churches will look differently from the typical, established church of the twentieth century. They will commit to the same functions (evangelism, worship, etc.) but will use different forms to accomplish them.

PART ONE

The Preparation for Developing a Strategy

Before one develops a strategy, some initial preparation is necessary. This preparation will lay a broad, general but critical foundation for the next section on process. Part 1 consists primarily of thinking through the need for and the importance, definition, and theology of the strategy. If leaders are not convinced of the need for and the importance of a strategy in their ministries, then ministry will not happen. But what is a strategy? Exactly what are we talking about? And, finally, is it biblical?

CHAPTER ONE

The Need for a Strategy

IS IT WORTH THE EFFORT?

"You see the trouble we are in: Jerusalem lies in ruins, and its gates have been burned with fire. Come, let us rebuild the wall of Jerusalem, and we will no longer be in disgrace."
—Nehemiah 2:17

It would not have been difficult to convince Pastor Robert Smith that he needed to develop a disciple-making strategy. You would not have needed to bend his arm behind his back nor twisted it a little. You may have resorted to some of these tactics with his board, but not with him. That does not mean that Faith Chapel Church did not have some kind of strategy. When Pastor Smith replaced his predecessor, he, like all other incoming pastors of established typical churches, inherited a strategy with a structure. There was already a structure in place that represented some kind of strategy. Otherwise the church would have been in chaos. The issue was: How good was that inherited strategy? The present strategy dated back to the founding of the church. The church's motto was: Come weal or come woe, our status is quo. The people greeted most attempts at change with the words, "If it ain't broke, don't fix it!" The problem is that the current strategy was broken and had been for a long time.

———————

Before you develop a strategy, at least a significant, high-impact strategy, you should be soundly convinced that you need one or else it will only be a halfhearted attempt at best. Otherwise, the final ministry strategy, once you complete it, will spend the rest of its life in the church filing cabinet somewhere under "s." Everyone will breath a sigh of relief and ask, "Now that that's out of the way, what's next?" And the familiar cliché "Someone convinced against his will is of the same opinion still" is true in the church world as well as life in general.

An important question must be asked: Is Faith Chapel typical or an anomaly as far as churches go? Are most churches across America thriving, whereas, only a few are like Faith Chapel? Have any others been left behind to minister as if American culture is still much as it was in the 1940s and 1950s? General statistics on the church as a whole and statistics on evangelism, discipleship, and pastor's concerns in particular indicate that Faith Chapel is typical.

GENERAL STATISTICS ON THE CHURCH

The life cycle of a church begins when it is born or planted (fig. 1.1). In most situations, the church grows for a time until it hits various growth barriers. The two most prominent barriers the church faces are at around two hundred and eight hundred people, although few churches grow to the point where they have to face the latter. Regardless, the church will grow until it hits a growth barrier, at which time it plateaus. Some churches through careful planning fight through the plateau and resume their normal growth pattern. However, other churches remain on the plateau and in time begin to decline or die. This is the story of Faith Chapel Church.

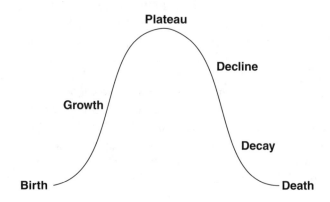

Figure 1.1 Church Life Cycles

General statistics on the church in North America indicate that it has not done well at making disciples in the latter half of the twentieth century. According to church growth consultant Win Arn, 80 to 85 percent of churches across America are plateaued or in decline.[1] Of the 15 to 20 percent that are growing, most is the result of transfer growth, not conversion growth. Lyle Schaller in commenting on the older American churches writes that "two-thirds to three-fourths of all congregations founded before 1960 are either on a plateau in size or shrinking in numbers."[2]

One pollster is more optimistic and believes that the idea that church growth has plateaued or declined is a myth. He writes:

> The statistics we have available also point out that while growth has been relatively slim during the past five years, most churches have grown. Once again, this shatters the prevailing myth that most churches are plateaued or in decline. Overall, 65 percent of the churches provided statistics that indicated growth in worship attendance.[3]

However, he further adds: "Before we become too enthralled, we should realize that in most cases this was single-digit growth. Less than one out of every five churches grew by 10 percent or more during 1987 to 1992 period."[4]

I have several problems with those who say that the idea that most churches are plateaued or in decline is a myth. First, my experience is that churches and pastors tend to over-report matters such as church growth. Ask most parishioners or visionary pastors about how their church is doing and most likely you will get a good report. This is not to say that they are intentionally attempting to mislead anyone. Instead, they are being optimists. They believe in what they are doing and in their churches. So they will tend to emphasize the positives and downplay the negatives. As a pastor, I know.

Second, a recent study indicates that people who respond to surveys such as those done by pollsters tend to overreport the facts. This study entitled "What the Polls Don't Show: A Closer Look at U.S. Church Attendance" by Hadaway, Marler, and Chaves was forthcoming in the *American Sociological Review*.[5] It was a response to a Gallup survey that indicated approximately 60 percent of America is unchurched. What this team did was to attempt a head count by traveling to Ashtabula County in Ohio. This study indicated that the percentage of unchurched was closer to 80 percent. Why the discrepancy between the poll and the actual head count? The interpretation is that people like to see and present themselves as better than they really are. Thus, the tendency is to exaggerate or overreport.[6]

Finally, if churches are in fact growing, although only slightly, what kind of growth are they experiencing? Some figures below will indicate that it is not conversion growth where lost people are being reached with the gospel. I believe that most churches will acknowledge this. Instead, the churches that are growing are mostly experiencing transfer or biological growth. Consequently, if people are moving from church to church (transfer growth) and having children (biological growth), then it would seem that each church is growing. However, the mark of a Great Commission, disciple-making church is conversion growth where unchurched people are becoming churched people with a passion for Christ.

STATISTICS IN PARTICULAR

The statistics on evangelism and discipleship indicate that the church is not making disciples.

Evangelism

When the church is struggling as it is at the end of the twentieth century, one of several ministry casualties is evangelism. Numerous reasons exist for the decline in evangelism. The question here is not why fewer churches are evangelistic but rather why is this so?

Bill Hull writes that according to a 1980 Gallup poll of the 22 million evangelicals who attend church, only 7 percent have taken any training in evangelism and only 2 percent have led someone to faith in Christ. He concludes: "The test of a congregation, apart from personal holiness, is how effectively members penetrate the world. American churches are filled with pew-filling, sermon tasting, spiritual schizophrenics, whose belief and behavior are not congruent."[7]

Bob Gilliam, the Director of Church Effectiveness for the Evangelical Free Church, has provided me with a survey that he conducted of more than 500 churches in 40 denominations over a ten-year period including more than 130,000 church members. It reveals that the average evangelical church led 1.7 people to Christ for each 100 people in attendance.[8] If an insurance company hired 100 salespeople, and they averaged 1.7 sales among them, then the company would not be in business for long.

A sample of churches like the above usually contains a number of smaller churches. Many assume that larger churches are doing a better job at evangelism—that is why they are large. However, Carl George writes that this is not the case.

> There exists a widespread notion that North America's medium- and large-size churches are evangelistic centers. This view is, in most cases, regrettably a myth. Instead, these churches are by and large centers for reprocessing believers, new and old alike, that throng to them from smaller churches.

This situation leads to one of the largest spiritual dilemmas of our time: The bigger a church becomes, the less evangelistically responsible it needs to be in order to grow.[9]

Finally, one writer notes that often there is a contradiction between what we say and do in response to our religious beliefs. For example, the vast majority of Americans share orthodox Christian beliefs such as the virgin birth, the death and resurrection of Christ, and miracles. However, apparently we do not believe them strongly enough to share our faith. Barna writes: "In the past seven years, the proportion of adults who have accepted Jesus Christ as personal Savior (34 percent) has not increased."[10]

Discipleship

Another ministry casualty is discipleship. The statistics and surveys on discipleship indicate that the American church is not making disciples.

In 1994, Bob Gilliam developed a survey he called the "Spiritual Journey Evaluation." This survey was an attempt to determine if the church today is making disciples according to Christ's criterion in Matthew 28:19–20. It asked people to evaluate themselves based on the very behaviors that Christ commanded of his disciples. Then it categorized them into four "training phases" that Christ took his disciples through. Gilliam elaborates these as follows: Phase 1 is salvation and commitment to growth; phase 2 is developing basic Christian habits; phase 3 is continued growth and discipling others; and phase 4 is continued growth and training disciple makers.[11]

Gilliam assumed that if churches were being intentional about Jesus' command and disciple making, then we could expect the following:

1. It would take most attendees no more than two or three times as long as Jesus' disciples to go through each phase of spiritual maturity.
2. There would be at least *some* correlation between the length of time persons had been Christians and their maturity level.
3. Most people would understand the meaning of the basic spiritual disciplines and the meaning of "a consistent *daily* time with God."
4. *Most* people in churches would be growing spiritually and changing their behavior to be more like Christ.[12]

This survey included almost 4000 attendees in 35 churches in several denominations scattered from Florida to Washington. After analyzing the results, Gilliam observed the following:

1. There is absolutely no correlation between the length of time a person has been a Christian and their level of maturity.
2. Many persons do not understand the meaning of discipleship or the spiritual disciplines. For instance, it is very common for people to report that they *did* have a regular *daily* time with God, but in a later question state that they only did this about twice a year.
3. Most people in these churches are not growing spiritually. Of those taking this survey, 24 percent indicated that their behavior was sliding backward and 41 percent said they were "static" in their spiritual growth.
4. Here is how the time Jesus took to train his disciples compares to the average time it takes church members to achieve the same maturity level.

	Jesus	**The Church**
Phase 1	3 months	18 years
Phase 2	9 months	18 years
Phase 3	2 years	21 years
Phase 4	2+ years	21+ years (avg. = 29 years)[13]

In answering the question: What does all this mean? Gilliam states that churches are not effectively being intentional about making disciples. These churches are not exceptions but are normative. He adds, "There is very little reason to believe that your church is any different!"[14]

These churches cannot be intentional about making disciples for the following six reasons:

1. Their leaders don't know what a disciple looks like.
2. They don't know how to make a disciple even if they can define one.
3. They don't know how church programs work together to make disciples.
4. They have no way to measure progress.
5. Their leaders are not model disciples but they do reproduce after their kind.
6. They didn't know how to become intentional without splitting the church![15]

David Dawson, who is the executive director of the Equipping the Saints Ministry and an experienced discipler, also wrestles with the reason why churches are not making disciples. Ultimately it is because so few churches have a strategy for making disciples. They are depending on a "more-caught-than-taught" strategy or what I call "discipleship by osmosis." They hope that somehow people will learn on their own. Dawson explains in the following:

> In my limited experience, it seemed to me that only a few people out of a hundred ever rose to the surface in a "more-caught-than-taught" system (the system used predominantly for training in most church and Christian organizations). The reason for this is that people who effectively learn in this system must be able to *analyze* what they both see and hear, *synthesize* the principles that provide the structure for what they've seen and heard, then package those principles into an "application," or usable tool. Finally, they need to *program* both the tool and the people into a course of study and train their people until the principles become reality in their lives. *I had often contended with my colleagues that only about five out of every one hundred people can do these things!* . . . When I discussed the validity of my observations with Dr. Howard Hendricks of Dallas Theological Seminary, he completely agreed, except for the fact that he felt only *two* of *one hundred* excel in this environment![16]

Instead, the church needs to work through the process, and develop a strategy for its people, rather than leaving it up to them.

Gilliam closes his survey with the question: What do we need to do? His answer is to overcome these obstacles and make disciples without splitting the church. This is the purpose of the very fine T-NET program developed by Bob and Bill Hull and offered through the Evangelical Free Church.[17]

In addition to Gilliam's survey, the majority of pastors feel that the church in America is having little disciple-making impact in general on individuals and society. Barna writes that 4 out of 10 pastors say that their present church experience is not significantly deepening their relationship with Christ and only 6 percent strongly believe American Christians are undergoing any kind of a spiritual renewal.[18] With an average tenure of four years, none said that seminary had prepared them well for the responsibilities of leadership they have encountered in their ministry.[19]

The question that remains is: Why is the church not fulfilling the post-Easter commission to make disciples? Bill Hull offers that "Christians are not well trained, largely because pastors have not worked out a means of helping people do what He (Jesus) has told them they should do. As a result they feel a great deal of frustration and guilt."[20] If you ask pastors why they do not help their people to become disciples, most answer that they do not know how. A typical response is: "Seminary taught me Greek, Hebrew, and theology, but no one taught me how to make disciples which is at the very heart of ministry!"

My opinion is that everyone needs to stop passing the buck and get down to the business of making disciples. The churches need to stop blaming the pastors. The pastors should stop blaming the seminaries. Instead, churches, pastors, and seminaries must become intentional about disciple making and work together to fulfill Christ's mandate for the church.

QUESTIONS FOR DISCUSSION AND REFLECTION

1. What does your church share with Faith Chapel Church? What does it not have in common? If you are a pastor, how can you identify with Pastor Robert Smith?

2. Where is your church on the ministry life cycle? Is it growing, plateaued, or in decline? Why? What about the other churches in your community?

3. Was your church born before or after 1960? If before, how does it compare with Lyle Schaller's statistic that two-thirds to three-fourths of all congregations born before 1960 are plateaued or in decline?

4. How is your church doing in terms of evangelism? How many people came to faith this past year as the result of the church's ministry? Of the number of people who join the church, what percentage is the result of evangelism? What percentage of the church's budget goes toward evangelism (not including world missions)?

5. How would you rate your church in terms of intentional disciple making? What does a disciple look like? Do you know how to make a disciple? How do your church's programs work together to make disciples? Does the church measure progress in its disciple-making efforts? If so, how?

6. If you are a leader in your church, do you feel that you are a model disciple? Has anyone ever discipled you? Have you ever discipled another person? Why or why not?

7. If your church sought to become intentional about making disciples, what would happen? Would it split the church? Why or why not?

8. Are you convinced that your church needs a disciple-making strategy or a better disciple-making strategy? Why? Why not?

ENDNOTES

1. Win Arn, *The Pastor's Manual for Effective Ministry* (Monrovia, Calif.: Church Growth, Inc., 1988), p. 16.

2. Randy Frazee with Lyle Schaller, *The Comeback Congregation* (Nashville: Abingdon Press, 1995), p. 11.

3. George Barna, *Today's Pastors* (Ventura, Calif.: Regal Books, 1993), p. 77.

4. Ibid.

5. C. Kirk Hadaway, Penny L. Marler, and Mark Chaves, "What the Polls Don't Show: A Closer Look at Church Attendance." Research Office, United Church Board for Homeland Studies, 700 Prospect Avenue, Cleveland, OH 44115.

6. Ibid., p. 12.

7. Bill Hull, *The Disciple Making Pastor* (Old Tappan, N.J.: Fleming H. Revell, 1988), p. 20.

8. Bob Gilliam, Church Development Survey, Denver Seminary.

9. Carl F. George, *The Coming Church Revolution* (Grand Rapids, Mich.: Fleming H. Revell, 1994), p. 38.

10. George Barna, *The Frog in the Kettle* (Ventura, Calif.: Regal Books, 1990), p. 115.

11. Bob Gilliam, "Are Most Churches Intentionally Making Disciples?" Findings from the "Spiritual Journey Evaluation," March 29, 1995, p. 1.

12. Ibid.

13. Ibid., p. 3.

14. Ibid.

15. Ibid.

16. David L. Dawson, *Equipping the Saints Introductory Guide*, 4400 Moulton Street, Suite D, Greenville, TX 75401, pp. 4–5.

17. If you are interested in more information about this program, contact the EFCA Training Network, 901 East 78th Street, Minneapolis, MN 55420.

18. George Barna, *Today's Pastors* (Ventura, Calif.: Regal Books, 1993), pp. 59, 69.

19. Ibid., pp. 26, 36, 126.

20. Hull, *The Disciple Making Pastor*, p. 20.

CHAPTER TWO

The Importance of a Strategy

WHAT DIFFERENCE WILL IT MAKE?

"Again, if the trumpet does not sound a clear call, who will get ready for battle?"   —1 Corinthians 14:8

No one needed to convince Pastor Robert Smith that Faith Chapel Church needed a strategy. One reason is that he also saw the importance of a fresh, significant strategy to the impact of Faith Chapel Church on its people and its community if it was to survive. The problem was convincing his people. Years of growing old together had its consequences. He compared establishing and growing a church to pouring concrete. By the time that he came to Faith Chapel, the church had long since established itself, and most minds were firmly set. When Smith thought about the church, often the picture of the proverbial ostrich with its head buried in the sand came to mind. Few of his people seemed to understand contemporary times, and most hoped somehow to preserve the past when life was so much more simple. Whenever he talked about such concepts as vision, mission, values, and strategy, most brows wrinkled and people asked: Why? Why do we need such things? He suspected that they were simply resisting any attempts at change.

Regardless of why the church is asking why, Robert Smith does owe his congregation an explanation. It is up to him to answer the *why* question. It is his responsibility to explain to and convince the people of the importance of a strategy, at least, a better strategy than the present unwritten one. There are no fewer than ten reasons why a carefully thought through strategy is so important to any ministry, whether a church or parachurch.

A STRATEGY ACCOMPLISHES THE MISSION

You may have the greatest mission in the world—to save the world, to feed the hungry, to heal the sick, to bring peace to all nations and people. Experts may examine your strategic mission and then step back and proclaim that you are an incredibly gifted genius and blessed by God. However, if you have no way to accomplish your mission, then essentially you and the others on your team are wasting your time.

Your strategy is the vehicle that enables the ministry or church to accomplish its mission or overall goal, which is the Great Commission (Matt. 28:19–20). It moves people from where they are spiritually (lost, immature) to where God wants them to be spiritually (mature disciples). A good strategy delivers, that is, it accomplishes the biblical, theological mission that is central and vital to the ministry.

Thus, a strategy puts feet on our theology. Most pastors and leaders know some theology and Bible, especially those who have attended a Bible college or seminary. Many have studied on their own. The problem is that they do not know how to implement their knowledge of the Bible and theology in the ministry. Seminaries are strong on the theoretical, but they give little help in the areas of mission, vision, and strategy development. Without a strategy, leaders find themselves in the same situation as Pastor Robert Smith. They have much, significant information with no delivery system, the consequence of which is massive frustration.

A STRATEGY FACILITATES UNDERSTANDING

If you were to take a quick tour of the churches all across the landscape, whether large or small, national or international, you would discover that the one thing they all have in common is programs, many programs. There are programs to minister to children, teach the Bible, pray, feed the poor, provide for the elderly, promote missions, and so on. In older churches the programs inside the facility have much in common with the paint on the outside of the facility: there are layers and layers of them, one on top of the other. No one has taken the time to remove the lower layers. They have simply accumulated over the years. Most often there is little rhyme or reason to them.

In his survey, Bob Gilliam discovered that most churches do not understand how their programs work together and what each contributes to accomplish the Great Commission or to make disciples. The truth is that many have lost their effectiveness and contribute little. In fact, some work against one another and can be counterproductive. For example, today most Christians with their crowded schedules attend a church-related event only once or at the most twice a week. However, many churches schedule two, three, or more events each week such as a Sunday school program, a Sunday morning worship service, a Sunday evening sermon, a Wednesday night prayer meeting, a children's program, a leadership meeting, and others as if their people would be present at most if not all of them. This forces people to choose what they will and will not attend. The church has not taken into account the busyness of its people nor thought strategically about which programs work together to make disciples.

Often the people who are involved in and vital to the church and its programs do not understand what they are doing or why they are doing it. Thus, they get little out of it spiritually. For example, many Christians attend a Sunday morning service that involves worship and a sermon. However, few understand the strategy behind this service and how it contributes to their spiritual growth and development. If you were to visit one of the services and ask the people why they are doing what they are doing, many would struggle with an answer. Some would answer that they are learning the Bible and spending time in prayer and worshipping God, while others would answer: "We've always done it this way."

The strategy is the thread that runs through all the programs and not only ties them together but communicates the spiritual purpose of each. That is a function of the strategy. First, you develop the strategy, then you program around it. The program is designed to accomplish some phase of the strategy. Thus, the strategy communicates to your people what they have to do to get where they want to go—the process—and precisely where they are in that process. And it communicates how the different programs work together to facilitate their spiritual development. If a program no longer contributes spiritually to the strategy or in some way detracts from it, then it is dropped. This promotes a lean and effective disciple-making program.

Strategic thinking results in good communication and understanding. In chapter 10, I have used a baseball diamond to illustrate a model strategy for a new paradigm church.[1] Each base represents a new and higher level of commitment for those who are moving from new birth to maturity. The idea is to move around the base paths or mature in Christ. Each base has programs that are designed to help people attain that level of maturity and commitment. Developing a strategy and communicating it similarly informs your people so that they know why you are doing what you are doing, and why they are doing what they are doing. They understand the strategy, where they fit into it, and the role each program or event plays in assisting them to accomplish the strategy. At any time they can tell you where they are in the disciple-making process. They are aware of their present level of spiritual commitment, a fact that encourages them. At the same time they know what the next level is, which provides them with a fresh challenge. All of this makes each program or event more meaningful.

A STRATEGY PROVIDES
A SENSE OF MOMENTUM AND PROGRESS

In his work, Bob Gilliam found that of the churches surveyed most people are not growing spiritually and seem to know it. For example, 24 percent said that their behavior was sliding backward and 41 percent said they were "static" in their spiritual growth. The tendency among some churches is to blame the people and accuse them of spiritual lethargy, and this is true in many cases. However, if a church does not have a carefully developed, well thought-through strategy that facilitates spiritual growth, and that is true of 95 to 97 percent of the churches in America, then the church must share some of the blame.

People sense that the church is not doing much for them spiritually, that not much is happening. Consequently, they are standing still in their spiritual development. This does not mean that the church does not have some programs for its people. Most churches provide sufficient programming except for some small churches that may not provide enough for their young people. The problem is that the programs are largely ineffective at making disciples. This has resulted in a number of Christians who transfer to larger churches that have a broader ministry menu.

Also, a significant number of Christians are growing disillusioned with their churches and are looking elsewhere to meet their deepest spiritual needs. They have expressed their disillusionment by dropping out of church. Consequently, while there is a growing number of unchurched lost people across North America, there is also a growing number of unchurched Christians as well.[2]

I am convinced that when a church implements a high-impact strategy for making disciples and communicates it clearly to its people, then they will respond positively. Some have adopted the illustration of the baseball diamond mentioned above. This illustration not only promotes an understanding of how the programs strategically work together to make authentic disciples, but it also communicates a sense of momentum or progress. People who become involved will sense that there is movement, that they are going somewhere spiritually, that they are indeed growing and maturing, not simply sitting and soaking. They understand that they are in process—the process of realizing their personal, spiritual mission, not just standing still or treading water or even in decline like so many today. They can measure their progress and see themselves making progress. They are not a part of the 65 percent who are going nowhere; they are a part of the 35 percent who are moving forward. On the one hand, they know where they have been, how far they have come, and how much they have grown. On the other hand, they know what they are still lacking and where they need to go to continue their spiritual development. This awareness is vital and promotes a sense of momentum in one's spiritual development.

A STRATEGY CONVEYS A SENSE OF SIGNIFICANCE

All of us, whether Christian or non-Christian, need a sense of self-esteem, that we matter, that we have value and worth as people living on planet earth (Matt. 12:11). We also need a sense of significance, that not only do we matter but that what we do matters, that our lives and what we do with them, whether at work or home, make a difference (Acts 13:36). We want to believe that we are not simply taking up space, but that someone will miss us when we are gone.

It was Pastor Smith's growing sense of insignificance—that he was not being used of God to make a difference at Faith Chapel—that motivated him to think about leaving the ministry and returning to the marketplace. Luke states the strategic significance of King David's life and his ministry in Acts 13, where he says that David was a man after God's own heart (v. 22) who accomplished God's purpose in his generation (vv. 36–37). Serious Christians want their lives to have impact. Like David, we not only want to be people after God's own heart (character), but we desire that our ministry epitaphs read that we, too, accomplished God's purpose in this our generation (contribution).

A strong sense of significance is especially needed today by everyone involved in the church at the end of the twentieth century. A considerable number of disillusioned Christians are dropping out because they do not feel that the church or what they are doing in the church really matters or has any significance. A disciple-making strategy shows that what we are doing with our lives in and outside the church is important to our spiritual development and that of our families while at the same time advancing the cause of Christ not only in our community but around the world. The church is responsible in the disciple-making process to make sure that each disciple knows his or her divine design where he or she can have the greatest ministry impact and function within that context for maximum effectiveness.

A STRATEGY EMBRACES POSITIVE CHANGE

America and most countries around the world at the end of the twentieth century and the dawn of the twenty-first century have experienced what I call accelerating megachange. Stanley Marcus writes, "The current generations have witnessed and participated in more change than any 10 previous generations combined."[3] In what is known now as the Information Age, it should not surprise us that one source argues that knowledge doubles every two years.[4] Information is one of the powerful forces that drives change. Pritchett and Pound write: "Get this. There was more information produced in the 30 years between 1965 and 1995 than was produced in the entire 5,000-year period from 3000 B.C. to 1965."[5] Another writes, "Today's world is a difficult place. Mankind has experienced more change in the past twenty years than in the 2,000 that preceded them."[6] I am convinced that the only constant in today's culture is death, taxes, and change.

America is exploding with change more than at any given time in its history. We are living in a decade of accelerating megachange. In the last twenty to thirty years, Western society in general and America in particular has nervously climbed on board the roller coaster of change only to discover that there is no way off, and there seems to be no end to the ride.

Change is happening regardless of what we do to prevent it, and it can either help the church or hurt it. For example, the invention of the computer and the technology that has sprung up around it has proved most beneficial. Desktop publishing alone has saved the church hours of labor and produced quality bulletins, newsletters, and so on. However, changes in the culture such as the decline in moral values or a declining community have proved harmful. The response of far too many churches to all this change has been to assume the position of the proverbial ostrich—to bury its head in the sand and wait ten to twenty years to see if the change is of God, only to find that it is too late, that they have missed an opportunity to serve God's purpose in their community.

A well-developed strategy helps us deal more effectively with that change. Strategy is deeply immersed in change. In fact, it is all about change for it involves planned change. A good strategy regularly conducts community audits to recognize, observe, and evaluate the changes that are taking place in the ministry's neighborhood. It keeps the church informed of and abreast of change. Because the church knows precisely where it is going and has a strategy to get there, it can evaluate this change and determine whether it will help or harm the church in its journey to accomplish its mission.

A STRATEGY HELPS
REALIZE A PREFERRED FUTURE

Throughout history, mankind has been fascinated with the future. He knows that if he can predict the future, then he can make billions, rule the world, and control all that takes place within it. Christians have also been fascinated with the future as demonstrated by their interest over the years in Bible prophecy. The fact is that while God knows the future and has revealed much of it through his prophets, we cannot predict the future outside of what he has chosen to reveal to us. We can learn from our past to take advantage of our future (that is one of the purposes for studying history), but we cannot know the future.

However, we can plan and creatively strategize and thus to a certain extent create our own future if those plans and strategies honor God and he chooses to honor them. When we fail to plan and strategize for the future of our ministries, we leave our churches and parachurch ministries open and vulnerable to outside forces and circumstances that could do serious damage to them, forces such as urban sprawl, crime, zoning, harmful technology, declining moral trends, the whims of a new generation, and so on. Ignoring these forces and failing to plan allows these external elements as well as the forces of the Evil One to dictate the church's future (Eph. 6:10–18).

A strategy and all the planning that goes into a good one, not some outside force, can help us to realize or achieve our preferred future. The church's preferred future is the realization of the Great Commission in its ministry community. Its mission is to make disciples of all who are within its reach. A church or any ministry that knows where it is going and has carefully thought through and developed a strategy to get there most likely will arrive there. However, the opposite is true as well. Not to strategize is almost a guarantee that except for the grace of God a ministry will not see its preferred future. It is comparable to a cruise ship adrift at sea that moves not according to a predetermined course but at the whims of the wind and the tides that swirl all around it.

A STRATEGY ENHANCES MINISTRY SUCCESS

A casual stroll though the local bookstore in any mall reveals numerous books on success and how practically anyone can be successful in today's fast-paced world. Of course, you will need to purchase a particular book for twenty to thirty dollars and practice diligently what its author proposes. He or she will void the warranty should you vary even slightly from the prescription or formula for success. But this should not matter. After all, if it worked for the author, surely it will work for you.

Most of this success has to do with achieving immediate personal fame and fortune during one's life here on earth. Just think about it—you could achieve instant name recognition with most consumers and your product could become an item in every household. However, be forewarned that there is little if any spiritual substance in many of these secular books, and often they teach ideas that contradict Scripture (1 Tim. 4:6–8). Many Christians are aware of this and tend to react negatively to these self-success and self-help books and to the idea of success itself. The term *success* is a instant "turnoff" for many believers because it has been used in such a negative context. However, when faced with the simple, basic question: Do we not want to be successful in making more and better disciples (Matt. 28:19), the answer is a resounding yesæof course we do! We must not allow a market that has abused the term *success* to turn us sour on the concept or the reality that we do indeed want to be successful at what Christ has called us to do. Let us be careful with the term but not avoid its use because we fear that some might get the wrong idea. After all, it is a biblical term (Neh. 1:11; 2:20).

The process of strategizing involves regularly conducting internal audits on how the church is progressing toward its mission and external audits on what is taking place in the ministry community. This helps the church to make needed adjustments and changes to remain relevant and in contact with its community as well as on the cutting edge. Thus, it directly affects the ministry's success. However, failure to strategize means that the ministry does not make the necessary adjustments to stay current and realize its vision. In time this affects the very survival of that ministry as so many plateaued and dying churches have discovered too late. On occasion, due to bad weather or an emergency, a cruise ship will have to alter its course in route to its destination. However, this is necessary for without those adjustments, it may not arrive at all.

A STRATEGY MAXIMIZES MINISTRY ENERGY

Every Sunday numerous plateaued and declining churches (perhaps 60 to 85 percent) go through the motions of church. The people faithfully show up and sit through Sunday school and church. They place an offering in the plate and then go home thinking: "I have done my thing for God this week." A small number (Gallup estimates around 10 percent) are involved in the actual, ongoing ministry of the church. They may teach, take the offering, work in the nursery, or function as greeters before the morning worship service. Some who are talented musically (and some who are not so talented) may perform or lead singing during the morning worship service.

While effective ministry does take place, without a strategy many accomplish little in terms of making authentic disciples. This does not mean that they are not sincere or that they are not hard workers. However, they are expending an enormous amount of ministry energy, much of which is wasted effort. It is comparable to the steam that comes from a hot cup of coffee on a cold winter's day. It appears for a moment and then evaporates into the air. The problem is that their efforts are misdirected. They do not know why they are doing what they are doing. Consequently, they are pouring all their energy into outdated programs that touch and attract no one to Christ.

A high-impact strategy, however, serves to harness all that wasted energy. It directs and redirects the church's efforts into action steps or programs and ministries that actually produce disciples. It moves the ministry in a new direction and supplies fresh energy for the organization. It also serves to re-energize those who may have abandoned hope in the church's former direction or lack thereof over the years.

A STRATEGY PROPERLY
INVESTS GOD'S RESOURCES

God's resources are his people. He has seen fit to use people to accomplish his purposes (Dan. 4:35). While he is not dependent on people to accomplish his will, he has sovereignly chosen to work through them to accomplish certain aspects of his will in our world. It was to his disciples and ultimately his church that he gave the Great Commission (Mark 16:14–15). And it was the church that preached the gospel, planted churches, and spread Christianity all over the known world. In particular, God uses his people's talents, time, and treasure in his service.

God is responsible for man's talents—the natural and God-given abilities that we all possess. He has created each person with a unique design for ministry (Job 10:8–9) that includes his or her talents. This design includes such talents as a person's natural and spiritual gifts. The natural gifts are those that God gives to all people when they are born. God provides believers with special spiritual gifts when they accept Christ (1 Cor. 12; Rom. 12). The design also includes passion and temperament.

Our passion is our God-given capacity to fervently pursue ministry to a particular group of people or a particular ministry itself. Temperament relates to our inborn behavioral characteristics. The point is that God has made all Christians for ministry (1 Pet. 4:10; 1 Cor. 12:7), and God delights in using his people according to their special designs to accomplish his ministry.[7]

God also uses people's time. Our time is his time—we must live as if it belongs to him not to us. He controls our time and provides just enough for us to accomplish his plans for us (Prov. 16:4). Therefore, we should never argue that we do not have enough time to accomplish ministry for him. He knows our schedules and would never expect us to do more than what we have time for.

Finally, God uses our treasure. All that we have is from him (2 Cor. 9:10). He richly supplies all our needs and blesses us with the finances necessary to subsist. Most important, he gives us the privilege and joy of investing financially in building his kingdom (2 Cor. 8–9).

However, to invest one's God-given resources in a church or ministry that is simply going through the motions and has given little thought or effort to making disciples is a poor investment at best. Some at Faith Chapel feel this way about their church. It is a sign of irresponsibility, not faithfulness, to invest God's resources in that which no longer accomplishes God's purpose. Would you invest in a business venture that insists on operating in the red? Then why is the church?

The solution is for Faith Chapel and all churches is to adopt Christ's mission for the church and then to develop a disciple-making strategy that will turn that mission into reality. A church that has taken the time to develop a well thought-through, effective strategy for making disciples is a wise investment of one's ministry resources. You know that the strategic-minded church will use your talents, time, and treasure for the advancement of Christ's kingdom. Your involvement in this kind of church is comparable to investing one's money in a business that reaps huge benefits for its investors. The strategy helps all involved in the ministry to direct their God-given resources most effectively and efficiently for the Savior.

A STRATEGY DISPLAYS WHAT GOD IS BLESSING

Church history demonstrates that God uses different methods and programs at various times in human history. The functions of the church such as worship, evangelism, prayer, teaching, community, and so on are timeless and eternal. However, the forms that these functions take in a particular culture at a specific time in history may vary. The method or program that expresses a ministry form is time-bound and, therefore, should be timely.

One example is the function of evangelism. Whether the church exists in the first century or the twenty-first century, it is responsible to evangelize. However, the particular form of evangelism or evangelistic method has varied tremendously from the first century to the twenty-first century. For example, God used the camp meeting in the middle 1800s in America as a form for evangelism. He has also used the public invitation combined with an altar call (a form that Charles Finney popularized) up through the 1940s and 1950s.

However, at the end of the twentieth century and the beginning of the twenty-first century, many of these forms or methods are no longer effective in reaching new generations of North Americans. Instead, God is using other methods of evangelism such as that found in Steve Sjogren's *Conspiracy of Kindness*. Sjogren advocates a form of evangelism that involves God's people in doing deeds of kindness for those outside the faith, expecting and accepting nothing in return. This grace approach to evangelism has proved most profitable because anyone in the church can do some deed of kindness whether mowing someone's yard, washing a car, painting a house, giving away a Coke, and so on. This evangelism form has proved timely because today's generation is most skeptical toward Christianity and believes that most pastors and churches are simply after their money. The Holy Spirit is using the church's acts of kindness with this generation to demolish their skepticism and open their callous hearts to the gospel.

Regardless the method, this knowledge of what God is blessing not only in evangelism but other functions such as worship, community, and so on has everything to do with strategy. In developing its strategy to accomplish its mission, every ministry must keep in touch with what God is blessing. They must keep their eyes open for new ministry paradigms. The knowledge of what God is blessing as well as what he is not currently blessing in their community will help churches to determine their present and future ministry strategies. For example, they may discover that it is time to change and update a number of their ministry forms so that they can implement new ones that are more ministry-effective. They can learn from one another as to the most effective means to minister, especially if they are in the same geographical area. If their circumstances are similar, they do not have to reinvent the proverbial ministry wheel.

SUMMARY

Ten Reasons Why a Strategy Is Important

1. It accomplishes the mission.
2. It facilitates understanding.
3. It provides a sense of momentum.
4. It conveys a sense of significance.
5. It embraces positive change.
6. It helps realize a preferred future.
7. It enhances ministry success.
8. It maximizes ministry energy.
9. It properly invests God's resources.
10. It displays what God is blessing.

QUESTIONS FOR DISCUSSION AND REFLECTION

1. Can you think of any other reasons why a strategy is important to your ministry? Is so, what are they?

2. Does your church or ministry have a strategy? If so, is it accomplishing your mission? Why or why not? If it is not, what will you do about it?

3. Do the people in your ministry understand the strategy and their part or role in the strategy? Are the church's programs that are a vital part of the strategy helping or hindering the realization of your mission? Do they work together to accomplish the vision?

4. Do the people in your church feel that they are going somewhere spiritually, that they are growing and maturing in Christ? If so, why? Or do they believe that they are treading water or in decline in their spiritual development? If so, why?

5. As the result of their involvement in the ministry, do the people in your church sense that their lives count for something important? Do they believe that what the church is doing in general and what they are doing in particular are making a difference for God's kingdom? If not, then why not?

6. How has change affected your ministry? Do you have a well-designed strategy in place that helps you to deal effectively with that change? Why or why not?

7. Is your ministry determining its own future according to God's

directives or is something other than the church determining the future? If the answer is something else, what is it? What must you do about this?

8. Does the use of the term *success* bother you? If so, why? Do you want your ministry to experience success? Explain. What role does a significant strategy play in realizing ministry success?

9. Is your ministry experiencing lots of wasted energy or is it maximizing people's energy? Why or why not? Would you agree that a well thought through strategy or a lack thereof is a major reason why?

10. Is your ministry best utilizing its people's talents, time, and treasure for the Savior? How do you know? How might a strategy be a factor here?

11. Are you aware of what ministry forms (methods, programs, and so on) God is blessing in your community? Why or why not? If you can, identify some? Have these become or will they become a vital part of your ministry's strategy? Why or why not?

ENDNOTES

1. I got the idea for this illustration from Rick Warren, the pastor of Saddleback Community Church in Mission Viejo, California. Rick has written a very fine book entitled *The Purpose Driven Church* (Grand Rapids, Mich.: Zondervan Publishing House, 1995).

2. For more information on America's unchurched Christians, see William D. Hendricks, *Exit Interviews* (Chicago: Moody Press, 1993).

3. Stanley Marcus, "Colliding with Change," *The Dallas Morning News*, August 12, 1995, p. 2G.

4. Frank B. Withrow, "Guest Editorial," T.H.E. Journal, September 1993, vol. 21, no. 3.

5. Price Pritchett and Ron Pound, *A Survival Guide to the Stress of Organizational Change* (Dallas, Tex.: Pritchett & Associates, Inc., 1995), p. 2.

6. Michael E. Gerber, *The E-Myth* (New York: HarperBusiness, 1986), p. 156.

7. See my book *Maximizing Your Effectiveness* (Grand Rapids, Mich.: Baker Book House, 1995) for more information on this important topic.

CHAPTER THREE

The Definition of a Strategy

WHAT ARE WE TALKING ABOUT?

It would seem wise to define our terms from the beginning so that we know that we're talking about the same thing!

Pastor Robert Smith was convinced that Faith Chapel Church needed to rethink its strategy or how it planned to implement its mission. He doubted that the board or anyone else had ever given it careful thought. With the passing of time and pastors, someone kept adding program after program to an already crowded agenda. Most important, they were not making disciples. There was no time to waste. He must move forward and help his church to prepare for ministry in the twenty-first century.

Pastor Smith called for a meeting of the board of deacons at which he challenged them to move ahead with him as together they developed a fresh disciple-making strategy for the church. He could tell by the look on his weathered face and the tone of his gravely voice that the head deacon was not happy with the proposal. The man probed him with numerous questions, many of which did not make sense. Smith sensed that his own blood pressure was rising as he fought to control his temper. Finally, the head deacon angrily blurted out: "We don't need none of that Madison Avenue marketing stuff around here. I would vote against turning our church into one of those new rock-and-roll churches!" With this, Pastor Smith realized that they were not talking about the same thing. He was discussing strategy while the head deacon was discussing marketing. While the two have some similarities, they are different concepts.

People like Pastor Smith and his head deacon often get into needless, heated arguments only to discover late in the conversation if at all that they are not talking about the same thing. It is not natural to stop and define terms. Most assume that they are talking or arguing about the same thing when more often than not, they are not. For centuries this has proved to be a major obstacle to good communication. For the sake of clarity and to prevent any possible misunderstanding, the purpose of this chapter is to stop and define the term *strategy* and how it is used in this book and the chapters that follow. First, I will define what I mean by strategy. Then to sharpen the definition even further, I will discuss what I do not mean by this term.

WHAT IS A STRATEGY?

The Definition of a Strategy

I define a strategy as the process that determines how you will accomplish the mission of the ministry. This definition contains three important concepts.

A Strategy Has a Mission or an Overall Goal

First, the strategy involves a mission. The mission or goal is at the very heart of a ministry because it is what God designed the organization to do—what it is supposed to accomplish—the ministry end. Without a clear, concise biblical mission the ministry is rendered impotent and lethargic. My experience in working with denominations and churches is that few have thought through and articulated a significant overarching goal or mission statement. Far too many churches are like a ship at sea with no clear destination. They do not seem to know where they are going so any port will do. And their strategy for getting there is just as vague.

I believe that a critical part of my ministry to the church at the end of the twentieth century and the beginning of the twenty-first century is to call it back to the basics. Someone tells the story of a major defeat that Coach Vince Lombardi's Green Bay Packers suffered at the hands of the Chicago Bears. This took place during the early days of Lombardi's illustrious career with the Packers. No sooner had they arrived back home and gotten off the bus, than Lombardi ordered all the players to meet on the practice field in full uniform. When all were present, he announced that, considering their miserable effort against the Bears, they would return to the basics. Holding it up for all to see, he announced: "Gentlemen, this is a football!"

I am convinced that if any ministry is to develop a disciple-making strategy, it must go back to the basics. The basics for the church begin not with a football, but with the mission of the church. What is it that the church is trying to accomplish? What is it supposed to do? What will the strategy attempt to accomplish? The mission or primary goal of the church ultimately is the Savior's Great Commission. It is to evangelize the lost and disciple the saved.

A Strategy Involves a Process

Second, a good strategy consists of a process. It is the process of moving people from spiritual prebirth to Christian maturity (Matt. 28:19–20; Eph. 4:12–13; Col 1:28; 2:6–7). This involves moving them from where they are (unbelief or immaturity) to where God wants them to be (spiritually mature). This process does not take place overnight for it is a lifelong journey toward maturity.

Scripture recognizes that people are at different places in their spiritual journeys (Matt. 13:18–23). The Savior recognized this diversity as he took his disciples from new birth to maturity. The strategy is such that the individual can fit in wherever he or she is on the spiritual journey without having to start over or jump ahead. Thus, to a certain extent it is tailor-made or custom designed for individuals. Regardless of where they are, it takes them to maturity or serving discipleship.

There are two ways of viewing this process. In one, we may view coming to faith in Christ as God's moving a lost person across a continuum from one extreme (no knowledge of Christ) to the other extreme (communication with God). Faith in Christ would take place somewhere in between. Engel's scale (see fig. 2.2 on page 46) represents this continuum well.[1]

I identify the period from the one extreme to faith as prebirth. The period from faith to communication with God is maturity or growing maturity. This scale is helpful because it shows us the path one follows in moving from one extreme to the other. The strategizing process follows this path.

Another way to view the process is in terms of levels of commitment. Any strategy must take into account at least three commitment levels (fig. 2.1).

Level 3: Committed

Level 2: Converted

Level 1: Unconverted

Figure 2.1

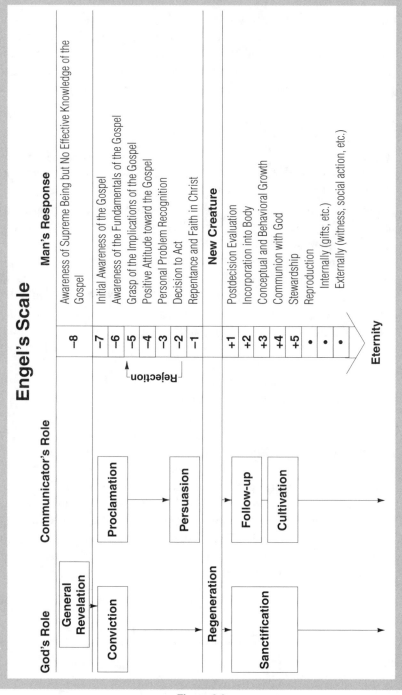

Engel's Scale

God's Role	Communicator's Role		Man's Response
		−8	Awareness of Supreme Being but No Effective Knowledge of the Gospel
	Proclamation	−7	Initial Awareness of the Gospel
		−6	Awareness of the Fundamentals of the Gospel
		−5	Grasp of the Implications of the Gospel
	Persuasion	−4	Positive Attitude toward the Gospel
		−3	Personal Problem Recognition
		−2	Decision to Act
General Revelation		−1	Repentance and Faith in Christ
Conviction			*Rejection*
Regeneration			**New Creature**
	Follow-up	+1	Postdecision Evaluation
		+2	Incorporation into Body
	Cultivation	+3	Conceptual and Behavioral Growth
		+4	Communion with God
Sanctification		+5	Stewardship
		•	Reproduction
		•	Internally (gifts, etc.)
		•	Externally (witness, social action, etc.)
			Eternity

Figure 2.2

Level 1 represents an unconverted person, level 2 is a converted person, and level 3 a committed Christian. The object of the church's strategy is twofold. First, it moves those at level 1 (the unconverted) to level 2 (converted) and then to level 3 (committed). Second, it takes those who are at level 2 (converted) and moves them to level 3 (committed). Commitment is crucial. Eighty to 85 percent of American churches are stuck in nominal Christianity (level 2). If these people fail to move on to level 3, then they soon will disappear in the quicksand of nominal Christianity.

A Strategy Answers the Question: How?

Third, a good strategy addresses a key question. It asks and answers: How will you achieve your mission? It is the overall process that helps a ministry accomplish what Christ has called it to do. It is the ministry means to accomplish the ministry end. For example, your mission may be to climb to the top of a mountain. The strategy is how you get from where you are to the top of that mountain—the action steps you take to get there.

Whether articulated or not, every ministry has a strategy. This is true of Faith Chapel Church, which has several Sunday school classes, a Sunday morning and evening service, and a Wednesday night prayer meeting. The very fact that a church is physically present at some location and does something for its people on Sunday morning means that it has a strategy. The question is: Is it a good one or a bad one? The answer has to do with whether the ministry is effectively accomplishing its mission. The "three to thrive" approach that has characterized Faith Chapel and so many churches in the twentieth century is not accomplishing the mission. It has not proved to be disciple-friendly.

The Kinds of Strategies

One aspect of defining a strategy should also include some discussion of the various kinds of strategies. We can further refine the definition of a strategy by examining the three different kinds of strategies.

The Personal Strategy

Every Christian is personally responsible to be one of Christ's disciples (Col. 2:6–7; John 13:34–35; 17:7–17). While Christ commands the church to make disciples, individual Christians must commit to become disciples. Each of us has an individual responsibility to grow and become a mature Christian.

I came to faith in Christ at age nineteen on the campus of the University of Florida in Gainesville, Florida. Unfortunately, no one offered to disciple me. That did not relieve me of my responsibility to pursue maturity. So I committed to the process by myself. The man who led me to faith in Christ taught a Bible study that I found very helpful. However, you cannot lecture people into maturity. I also read numerous pamphlets by Dr. M. R. De Haan of RBC Ministries in Grand Rapids, Michigan, explaining the Bible. I discipled myself.

I have been teaching at Dallas Theological Seminary for some fifteen years. Periodically, I survey my students by asking how many have ever been discipled or have discipled someone else. Except for those who have ministered with Campus Crusade for Christ or the Navigators, few can raise their hands. I suspect, however, that this is true of most if not all seminaries and Bible colleges that are training men and women for ministry. Not much discipleship is taking place in America at the end of the twentieth century.

Regardless, we are responsible for our own spiritual growth. This means that we must discover and adopt a personal strategy designed to move us from wherever we are spiritually to where God wants us to be, mature, Christlike Christians. If I had an opportunity to repeat my early spiritual life, I would work harder at finding someone to disciple me. However, there is an abundance of good material that is available that will help Christians to develop on their own. Any good Christian bookstore should have this material available or can order it for you.

The Corporate Strategy

The corporate strategy is the congregational or overall strategy that a ministry in general or a church in particular develops to help its people become disciples. It is also the primary topic of this book. Each Christian is individually responsible to become Christ's disciple, and the church is responsible to make disciples (Matt. 28:19). That means that the church is responsible to develop a corporate strategy that helps each of its members in the discipling process. It does everything possible to aid its people in accomplishing their personal responsibility—to be a disciple of Christ.

No one should have to "go it alone" as I and so many others have had to do. This points to a major breakdown in the churches with what they are supposed to be doing. The church should provide a disciple-making program that helps each believer to fulfill his or her individual responsibility to become a mature Christian.

The corporate strategy is also a vital part of a ministry plan or the planning document. The ministry plan is a broad general document that consists of several parts, one of which is the strategy. It comes after the values, vision, and mission statements. It is the process that tells how the ministry will accomplish its mission. The ministry's resources and structure follow and depend on it.

The Mini-Strategy

Not only will the ministry have a corporate strategy designed to help all of its people to become disciples, but each goal that makes up the overall strategy will have its own unique strategy to accomplish it. I refer to these as mini-strategies. The overall mission of the church has a congregational strategy, and each goal that is a part of that strategy will have its own mini-strategy that leads to its realization. Some commonly refer to these mini-strategies as methods, means, or vehicles.

For example, one of several goals in a church's strategy might be to grow people to spiritual maturity or to help their people become growing disciples. Every goal must have a strategy or better a mini-strategy or it will not happen. The mini-strategy to accomplish this goal is the implementation of discipleship small groups or fully functioning communities.

WHAT A STRATEGY IS NOT

Often people confuse the strategy with other ministry or planning concepts. Therefore, we can gain a greater understanding of the concept itself by distinguishing it from those concepts.

A Strategy Is Not a Mission Statement

Some writers confuse the mission and strategy. For example, one secular writer defines strategy as the nature and direction of the organization, its basic purpose. However, this confuses the mission with the strategy. The mission is what the ministry organization is to accomplish. It concerns the very nature and direction of the organization. The strategy affects how the organization accomplishes the mission.

The sport of mountain climbing provides an excellent analogy that illustrates and distinguishes the mission statement and other ministry concepts from the strategy. Using the mountain climbing metaphor, the mission is simply to get to or arrive at the top of the mountain safely. However, the strategy is what gets you to the top of the mountain. It consists of the action steps taken along the way that make it possible for you to even reach the peak.

A Strategy Is Not a Vision Statement

Another similar concept to the mission statement is the vision statement. The mission statement is primarily a planning concept. It identifies the ministry organization's direction and breaks down into the major goals around which it is structured. For example, a simple statement of the mission or overall goal of the church is to make disciples. The leader might break this mission or overall goal into four major goals for the church, such as to interest in becoming a disciple, to become a disciple, to become a growing disciple, and finally to become a serving disciple. The leader could then structure the entire church around these four goals. I will say more about this concept later in this book.

The vision statement, however, is a communication tool, not a planning tool. A speaker or preacher may cast a vision from the pulpit although there are numerous other ways to communicate vision.[2] Like the mission statement, it also identifies the organization's direction, but it is a seeing concept and it is usually much longer than a mission statement. It serves to help those within the ministry to catch a picture of the future of that ministry in their heads. It is what they see when they close their eyes and envision the church, two years, five years, ten years, even twenty years from the present.

The vision is what you see when you picture yourself standing at the top of the mountain even before you start the climb. It is a mental snapshot of you and the others in the expedition, proudly standing at the top with your arms around one another and snow all over the place. It serves to motivate and excite you about attempting the climb. Again, the strategy is the process that helps you to realize the vision, that gets you to the top. Nanus writes that "a strategy has cohesion and legitimacy only in the context of a clearly articulated and widely shared vision of the future."[3]

A Strategy Is Not Core Values

Core values explain why you do what you do. A ministry's core values are its constant, passionate, biblical beliefs that drive the organization. For example, a list of the Jerusalem church's core values is found in Acts 2:42–47. They consist of such values as the apostles' teaching, fellowship, the breaking of bread, and prayer. The vision and mission statements are *what* you do. The vision and mission statements serve to focus the church in terms of its direction, while the values drive or move the ministry in that direction.

The strategy is *how* you do what you do. The early church's strategy for accomplishing Christ's Great Commission is found in the Book of

Acts, particularly the missionary journeys or better the church planting journeys found in Acts 13:1–21:26. Your core values dictate why you are climbing to the top of the mountain in the first place. They drive every decision you make and every dollar you spend on the way to the top. The strategy provides the framework for getting to the top. It is imperative that the ministry strategy be consistent with its values. In *Shaping Strategic Planning*, the authors write: "Strategic management involves the execution of an explicit strategic plan that is consistent with the values and beliefs of those people who must execute it. . . ."[4]

A Strategy Is Not a Team

A team best accomplishes any kind of ministry. New Testament ministry is a team ministry. For example, Christ chose to minister through a team. Though he is God and the all-powerful Creator of the universe, he chose not to minister alone. Instead, he chose a band of fallible, often inept disciples (Mark 6:7) to work with him, who, in turn, turned the world upside down. Paul also ministered through a team. Initially, he partnered with Barnabas (Acts 11:22–30). At the end of his ministry he had recruited a rather large team of disciples such as Erastus, Gaius, Aristarchus, Sopater, Secundus, and Tychicus.

The team answers the question: *Who* is climbing to the top of the mountain? Who makes up the team that will attempt to make it all the way up the side of the mountain? The team is primarily responsible to develop the strategy; consequently, it is a tool of the team. The team should have a strategy or it is not likely that they will climb the mountain. The strategy also includes the team who will accomplish it and has had much to do with their selection, but it is not equated with the team itself.

A Strategy Is Not a Plan

Though it is common to equate a plan with a strategy, a strategy is not a plan as I have hinted above. Instead, a strategy is a part of a plan, and a good plan is part of the management process.[5] A plan has at least the following eight parts:

1. A statement of need
2. A mission (overall goal)
3. A vision
4. Core values
5. A strategy

6. Resources (personnel and finances)
7. A schedule (calendar)
8. Evaluation

Note that in this planning model, the strategy is the fifth part of the entire plan. Thus, the strategy is only one part of the bigger picture—the total plan. However, it is the action part. A strategy proposes specific courses of action.

The plan asks: How do you hope (or plan) to get to the top of the mountain? In some ways it is similar to the strategy but different from the strategy. It is similar in that both ask and answer the how question. This makes the two confusing. The plan is different in that it will not take you to the top of the mountain. It is more an intellectual exercise— a dream—that consists of your intention to make it all the way to the top.

In contrast, the strategy is not intention-oriented, it is action-oriented. The plan is a plan for action, whereas, a strategy is a specific course of action. A plan consists of goals and objectives. The strategy accomplishes those goals and objectives. Strategy is all about implementation and achievement. Again, the plan precedes the strategy, and the strategy is a part of the overall plan.

In *Managing the Non-Profit Organization*, Peter Drucker makes a distinction between a plan and a strategy. He affirms that the plan is intention-oriented, whereas, the strategy is action-oriented. He illustrates this distinction by quoting an old saying: "Good intentions don't move mountains, bulldozers do."[6] The mission and plan are good intentions; strategies are the bulldozers.

Drucker further clarifies that planning is what you want to do. It is an intellectual exercise—good intentions. The problem is that you will most likely put it in a nicely bound volume that winds up on your bookshelf.

Strategy, however, is not what you want to do but what you really do—your accomplishments. It is action-focused. It converts intentions into actions and busyness into work. It involves not wanting to do something but doing it. It is not something you hope for but something you work for.[7]

The distinction between a plan and a strategy is important because people commonly confuse the two. An example is Burt Nanus, who in *Visionary Leadership* equates the strategy with a pattern or plan.[8] Some use the term *strategic* as an adjective preceding plan. Kanter writes: "While 'strategic' is clearly an overused word, and many companies are dropping it as an automatic modifier to 'planning,' it does express an important idea for this part of the change process: deliberate and conscious articulation of a direction."[9]

In summary, it would appear that both the literature on the subject and the marketplace have used the term *strategy* rather casually. In fact, it has assumed a wide variety of meanings that serve only to confuse the *what* and *how* of the organization.

A Strategy Is Not Tactics

Whereas the strategy is the overarching process, the tactics are the decisions that make up and contribute to that process. They are the day-to-day and month-to-month decisions you make as you implement the disciple-making plan—the choices you make along the way as you exercise the strategy.[10]

The mountain climbing metaphor helps here. You have to make numerous decisions as you scale a mountain: Who will climb the mountain? When and how often do we stop and rest? At what times will we climb? How much water should we drink? Is a piece of equipment really safe or should we replace it? Is the rope tied well enough? Do we have the best boots for mountain climbing? and so on.

In ministry the tactics are the numerous day-to-day, week-to-week, and month-to-month decisions that someone has to make about the church as it follows its strategy to accomplish its mission. What will be the worship theme for the next series of sermons? Do we need to go to two services before or after the summer months? What kinds of small groups will we implement? What is the best disciple-making curriculum for our church? It is obvious that these issues are all important to the strategy. However, they are a part of the strategy and do not equal the strategy.

A Strategy Is Not a Structure

Structure has to do with organization. It is the way we organize our ministry team (staff, board, serving lay persons, and so on), and how those on the team relate to one another as they accomplish the strategy. It includes the lines of authority and communication between the different departments or ministries and the individuals within them. In short, it has much to do with how you arrange the "boxes" on a corporate or congregational organization chart. It answers such questions as: Who is on the team? Who is in charge? Who works for and reports to whom? Who is working together? What are the boundaries? It may also include the information that flows through the lines of authority and lines of communication.[11] A common mistake that leaders make when something goes wrong is to change the structure. They attempt to reorganize the organization when the problems lie much deeper, often at a core values and/or strategy level.

Structure normally follows strategy. For example, Nehemiah seems to have had a strategy in mind before he rallied the men and women together into a structure. He took the time to study the situation (Jerusalem's broken-down walls and gates) and then develop a strategy (Neh. 2:12–17). The strategy led to the structure that he implements in Nehemiah 3.

In our climb up the mountain, one person is the leader and guide. Another reports to him and is an expert with maps. Others simply carry the supplies. Each makes a separate but significant contribution in our climb to the top. The same applies to ministry. For example, the pastor is responsible for the staff and has the authority to recruit, hire, and lead them. They also report to him. However, he reports to the board. Some pastors work with an executive pastor. This is a person who oversees the rest of the staff but reports to the senior pastor. Larger churches often use this arrangement because it frees up the busy senior pastor from the day-to-day supervision of the staff so that he is free to do other things. Regardless, all have to do with a ministry's structure.

A Strategy Is Not Marketing

The term *marketing* has conjured up images of Madison Avenue and slick promotional schemes. Some unscrupulous businesses attempt in every way to sell poor, unsuspecting people products that they do not need, cannot afford, or really want. This false image is what the head deacon at Faith Chapel Church was responding to so negatively. In *Marketing the Church*, Barna shows how this is a mistaken image and how marketing practices, when properly understood, can help churches to accomplish the Great Commission and reach people.

Many churches in the late twentieth century have realized this and begun to use marketing principles to help their churches reach lost people. But there has been some confusion of marketing with strategy. We must not equate marketing with strategy. It includes strategy but is not the same as strategy. Like planning, it is bigger than a strategy. According to Barna, marketing is a process that involves "a broad range of activities such as research, product positioning, awareness development, strategic planning, pricing, advertising, public relations, and audience segmentation."[12] That it includes strategic planning means that it includes a strategy as every good plan must have one. Thus, strategy is a part of marketing since it is also an aspect of planning.

THE TEST OF A GOOD STRATEGY

1. Does the strategy have a biblical mission?
2. Is the strategy a process that moves people from spiritual prebirth to maturity?
3. Does the strategy clearly explain how the ministry will accomplish its mission?

QUESTIONS FOR DISCUSSION AND REFLECTION

1. Does your ministry have a mission? If it does not, then it will need to develop one before you can design a strategy. If it does, has it articulated this mission in some kind of mission statement? Is it a biblical mission statement?

2. A strategy moves people from prebirth to maturity. Does your ministry move people from prebirth to maturity? If so, how? (Examine your programs.) Do you feel that your present strategy is adequate, or do you need to rethink it? Why or why not?

3. Do you have a personal strategy to move yourself from prebirth to maturity? Is it adequate? Why or why not? Does your church have a disciple-making strategy in place to assist you in this process? If yes, what is it? If no, why not?

4. Does your ministry make a distinction between the strategy and the mission statement and/or the vision statement? If so, what is it? If not, why not?

5. Has your church articulated its core values? If not, why not? If so, are they viewed the same as or different from the strategy?

6. Does your church have a major planning document? If not, why not? Does the church also have a strategy? If so, does the church equate the strategy with the plan or is the strategy a part of the overall plan? What is the difference between a plan and a strategy according to this chapter?

7. Every church has a structure as well as a strategy. Does your ministry distinguish between the two? What is the structure of your church? (Describe or detail it.) Is the structure adequate to facilitate the strategy? Why or why not?

8. How do you and/or the people in your ministry react to the term *marketing*? What is the difference between marketing and a strategy? How have you attempted to market your church? How is this different from developing a strategy to make disciples?

ENDNOTES

1. James F. Engel and H. Wilbert Norton, *What's Gone Wrong with the Harvest?* (Grand Rapids, Mich.: Zondervan Publishing House, 1975), p. 45.

2. See Aubrey Malphurs, *Developing a Vision for Ministry in the 21st Century* (Grand Rapids, Mich.: Baker Book House, 1992), chap. 5.

3. Burt Nanus, *Visionary Leadership* (San Francisco: Jossey-Bass Publishers, 1992), p. 30.

4. J. William Pfeiffer, Leonard D. Goldstein, and Timothy M. Nolan, *Shaping Strategic Planning* (Glenview, Ill.: Scott, Foresman, and Company, 1989), p. 253.

5. The management process is made up of three phases: planning, organizing (structure), and controlling.

6. Peter F. Drucker, *Managing the Non-Profit Organization* (New York: HarperCollins Publishers, 1990), p. 59.

7. Ibid.

8. Nanus, *Visionary Leadership*, p. 54.

9. Rosabeth Moss Kanter, *The Change Masters* (New York: Simon and Schuster, 1983), p. 294.

10. See James C. Collins and William C. Lazier, *Beyond Entrepreneurship* (Englewood Cliffs, N.J.: Prentice Hall, 1992), pp. 95, 98.

11. See Alfred D. Chandler, Jr., *Strategy and Structure* (Cambridge, Mass.: The M.I.T. Press, 1962), pp. 13–14.

12. George Barna, *Marketing the Church: What They Never Taught You about Church Growth* (Colorado Springs, Colo.: NavPress, 1988), p. 41.

CHAPTER FOUR

The Theology of Strategy

IS IT BIBLICAL?

"In his heart a man plans his course, but the LORD determines his steps." —Proverbs 16:19

There was little doubt in Pastor Smith's mind that his church needed to rethink its strategy. However, he had attended an evangelical seminary that had thoroughly trained him in the Scriptures. He took courses on Bible, theology, and hermeneutics. He also had a working knowledge of Greek and Hebrew and could still sight read much of the New Testament from the original language. Consequently, in the deep recesses of his mind, he wondered if the whole concept of planning in general and strategizing in particular was biblical. He also questioned what it meant for something to be biblical. Does that mean that you have to find it or an example of it in the Bible before you can do it? One man on his board had graduated from a Bible college and was of that opinion. He wanted to know where the Bible taught that a church needs to develop a strategy. Pastor Smith was not prepared for this. So he began to study his Bible to resolve some of these issues.

———

While the importance of a carefully thought-through strategy is both logical and obvious, what do the Scriptures have to say about this concept, if anything? Do they have to? Since this part of the book (chaps. 1–4) lays a broad, critical foundation for the rest of the book, we should examine the theological basis for the concepts of planning and strategy. This chapter looks at two aspects of the biblical theological basis for developing a strategy. The first is the theology of change and the second is the theology of strategy.

THE THEOLOGY OF CHANGE

Strategy has everything to do with change. It involves constant, planned change. As the culture changes around the church, the latter must evaluate that change and make adjustments in its strategy to deal with that change. Consequently, a theology of strategy begins with and is affected by a biblical theology of change. Critical to a theology of change are the principles of function, form, and freedom (the three Fs).

The Principle of Function

The functions of ministry form the basis for which the ministry, whether church or parachurch, exists. They make up *what* the church does. The evangelical church properly contends that these functions must be derived from the Scriptures because they are biblical principles. Some examples of these functions are evangelism, worship, prayer, the communication or proclamation of the Word (preaching and teaching), confession, community, giving, discipleship, fellowship, leadership, discipline, and others.

Since these functions are based on Scripture, they are fixed and timeless, or eternal. They must never change. They are to be found in the twenty-first-century church as well as the first-century church. Christ's church will forever seek to base its ministry on them. Essentially, they form the core ingredients that make up any ministries of the church.

Churches of liberal theological persuasion differ with evangelical churches on this issue. They do not view the Bible as teaching eternal and binding truth for Christians, whether they lived in the first century or the twenty-first century. Consequently, they have responded to change and attempted to remain culturally relevant by either changing or abandoning the functions of the faith. For example, many liberal churches believe in evangelism but mean something other than preaching the gospel and leading people to faith in Christ. They have abandoned this concept and changed it to mean other things such as helping the oppressed and politically disenfranchised regain their God-given rights, and so on.

The Principle of Form

An Explanation of the Concept of Form

The forms of ministry are built on the functions of ministry. The forms are how the functions are expressed or accomplished in ministry. Whereas the functions are *what* the church does, the forms affect *how* and even *when* a church does *what* it does. For example, evangelism is a ministry function that is essential to every church. However, evangelism can and should take different forms. Those with the gift of evangelism often use a confrontational style. Others prefer a more relational style such as friendship evangelism. I have discovered that one's style of evangelism depends mainly on his or her temperament.[1]

The forms are time bound and thus temporary—they are changeable and not fixed. They should be changed or adjusted so that the ministry remains relevant to its community. The New Testament writers give us little information on the forms of the early churches (1 Cor. 14:22–40) and what information is available is more descriptive than mandated. In 1 Corinthians 14:22–40, Paul did not tell the church at Corinth how to worship; he only directed them to conduct their public worship in a "fitting and orderly way," an instruction that holds true in any century.

I believe that the scant information given to us on ministry forms in the first century may have been intentional so that later churches would not lock into first-century forms. We do not have to do ministry the way they did it in the early church. The question here is: What way was that? It appears that the various New Testament churches ministered in different ways using different forms. Instead, God intentionally gives the church freedom to determine the forms that the functions take.

It is in the area of form that theological liberalism also failed. Liberals changed the functions that formerly were based on biblical principles but held to their same old forms and traditions. In essence, they reversed the process and are paying an evident price—mainline liberal churches are in serious decline. On the one hand, they have very little theological substance. On the other hand, to visit some of their churches is to discover what life was like in the typical church in the 1930s and 1940s. They, like many evangelical churches, have not changed much in *how* they do *what* they do.

Form and Tradition

Another critical area under the topic of form is tradition. Traditions are forms that have become relatively fixed over the years. They are nonbiblical forms, either good or bad, that one generation passes on to another. Good traditions do not detract from Scripture. For example, Christ's custom of going into the synagogue and standing up to read (Luke 4:16) or Paul's custom of going first to the synagogue and reasoning with the Jews from the Scriptures (Acts 17:2) were traditions that did not detract them or their audience from the clear teaching and functions of Scripture.

Some people have confused their traditions with biblical teaching. The Pharisees were guilty of this in Jesus' day when they placed the ceremonial washing of hands as equal to or above Scripture (Matt. 7:1–23). Many people in our churches assume that the Bible teaches their traditions as the way we have to do ministry. When asked about why the church practices a certain tradition, they respond that they have always done it that way and assume the reason is that somewhere the Bible says that you are supposed to do it that way. This is especially convenient for those who resist or fear change. While most traditions may be good and were effective at some time, clinging to those traditions and refusing to change them when they are no longer relevant or ministry-effective is bad. This results in putting tradition before Scripture (Mark 7:1–13).

Another problem is that not only will a generation confuse their traditions with Scripture, but they will attempt to impose their traditions on another, often younger, generation. This has largely taken place most recently in North American Christianity in the middle to late twentieth century. The results have been disastrous for many of those in the younger generations who have responded by dropping out of church. Kennon Callahan writes, "New understanding of doing ministry (praxis) must be created with each new generation for the church's mission to move forward. When an older generation imposes its understanding on the new generation—however innocently—both groupings become dysfunctional. Each new generation must carve out an understanding of ministry that matches its time."[2]

The Principle of Freedom

An Explanation of the Concept of Freedom

Actually, much of what we do in church, perhaps as much as 90 to 95 percent, we base on culture not Scripture. I am talking about the forms or traditions—the ways in which we have become accustomed to doing church: choirs, hymnals, musical instruments, formal clothing, the order of worship, even the day of worship, and so on. I also believe that this was true of the church in the first century as well as the church of today.

This does not mean that what churches are doing is wrong or unbiblical. What it does mean is that the church has freedom to change and must change to stay relevant and to prepare itself for ministry in the twenty-first century. Francis Schaeffer wrote: "Not being able, as times change, to change under the Holy Spirit is ugly. The same applies to church polity and practice. In a rapidly changing age like ours, an age of total upheaval, to make nonabsolutes absolutes guarantees both the isolation and death of the institutional, organized church."[3]

Scripture has a liberating or freeing effect (James 1:25; 2:12; John 8:31–32). Since the Bible does not set the forms, the church may and should change them to best reach those in our culture without violating the functions of Scripture. We dare not make the mistake of the Amish who, in an attempt to preserve their traditions, have locked themselves into an eighteenth-century culture. They have not incorporated a biblical culture but have made the culture of the eighteenth century their church culture and have resisted all attempts at change. Consequently, they have had little, if any, impact in terms of being salt and light (Matt. 5:13, 14) to a lost and dying world in the twenty-first century. Some would have the evangelical church of the late twentieth century retreat into the culture of the first century in similar fashion.

Contextualization versus Accommodation

The struggle for the church in the area of freedom will always be contextualization versus accommodation or compromise. On the one hand, are you biblically applying the Scriptures to the community and culture in which your church ministers (contextualization), or are you unbiblically conforming to the culture—buying into the spirit of the age and its trends and fads and thus compromising (accommodation)? A similar but different question is: Are you relevant to the culture but not distinct from it, or are you not relevant to the culture but distinct from it (as the Amish and others)? Both of these latter questions relate to the concept of separation, and neither is a biblical position. Christ's church at any time walks a fine line between these two extremes. To slip in either direction is to risk the spiritual and institutional death of the ministry organization. Therefore, today's pastors must not only practice sound, biblical hermeneutics in regard to doctrine but must also understand how that doctrine relates to living in a particular culture at a particular time.

Hermeneutical Issues

There are two hermeneutical principles some attempt to follow that are misleading and have caused problems in determining what the church can and cannot do. In an attempt to help the church follow biblical guidelines, both principles have captured and to some extent gobbled up biblical freedom (James 1:25; 2:12).

The first is the negative hermeneutic. It teaches that unless you can find a particular form or practice within the pages of the Bible it is wrong and you cannot do it. Some communicate this view with such clichés as "Where the Bible speaks, we speak, where the Bible is silent, we are silent." For example, I once heard a well-known Bible expositor teach that contemporary drama as used in a number of the contemporary churches is not found in the Bible and therefore should not be found in the church. He argued that drama was common in the first century among both the Greek and the Roman cultures, and since the churches recorded in Acts chose not to incorporate drama into their services, then it is wrong for us to do so today.

There are two problems with this view and those similar to it. First, much of what most churches are doing today as well as throughout church history is not found in the pages of the Bible. This is true of the use of organs and pianos, hymns, the Sunday school, a pulpit, church buses, microphones, the altar, flowers, the baptistery, and so on. These are all a part of the culture of today's church, yet few condemn their use. According to the logic of the negative hermeneutic, however, these practices and traditions are unbiblical and should not be found in the church that names the name of Christ. However, the same expositor strongly favored most, if not all, of these forms. I find this position not only unbiblical but inconsistent.

The other problem with this view is that just because the churches in the book of Acts and the rest of the New Testament do not mention drama, does not mean that those churches did not use drama or did not choose to use it in their services. Also, it is possible that other churches in the first century that are not mentioned did use them. Absence of proof is not proof of absence. This is a matter of silence. We simply do not have much information on what the churches of the first century did and did not practice. It is just as reasonable to argue that God in his wisdom was trying to protect his church from the inconsistencies of the negative hermeneutic!

A second view is patternism. This view builds on the first and teaches that the way the New Testament church did something is how the church must do it at all times and in all places. The church's forms or practices, especially if it does them repeatedly, are as binding as its functions. For example, some believe that the church must observe the Lord's Supper weekly. They base this on Acts 20:7 that says: "On the first day of the week we came together to break bread." However, there are several problems with this interpretation. First, the text does not indicate that this was a regular practice. Second, it describes what the church did, but does not mandate that it be done weekly. Finally, in 1 Corinthians 11:24–25 Paul mandates the observance of the Lord's Supper, but in verse 26 seems to leave the frequency of observance open with the use of the words "whenever you eat this bread and drink this cup. . . ."

The problem is that this view rests on what I refer to as descriptive passages, not prescriptive. The former are sections found in the Scriptures that describe forms or practices of the early church. Simply because the Scriptures describe what the first-century church did repeatedly, does not necessarily mean that today's church has to follow those patterns. The latter, prescriptive passages, are the commands found in the text. The biblical imperatives are another matter. If the New Testament mandates an observance such as the Lord's Supper (Matt. 26:26–27; 1 Cor. 11:24–25), then the church must observe it. This is not a matter of freedom. However, a word of caution is important here as well because it does not always follow that the church practices every imperative today. For example, Romans 16:16 commands; "Greet one another with a holy kiss"! Wisely perhaps, few churches practice this command in the contemporary church.

Further, we do not necessarily know how all the churches accomplished functions such as worship. We have some idea of how the church at Corinth practiced worship from 1 Corinthians 14. However, there is no indication that the other churches such as Jerusalem, Antioch, Rome, Ephesus, Derbe, and Lystra followed this format. Thus, different churches may have worshipped in different ways. Which are we to follow?

Both these hermeneutical principles serve to goad us to rethink what we mean when we ask if something is biblical or unbiblical. What do we mean? Do we have to find something somewhere in the Bible (a proof text) before we can do it? If you cannot find something in the Bible, could it still be biblical and thus true and appropriate for ministry? I would argue that in discussions of what is biblical or unbiblical, the key is that something agrees or disagrees with the Bible, not that it is either present or missing from the text of the Bible.

THE THEOLOGY OF STRATEGY

Any theology of strategy begins with a theology of change because strategy has everything to do with change. It continues, however, with an examination of some of the numerous examples of strategy found both in the Old and New Testaments. Also, it must conform with other theological truths such as the sovereignty of God, dependence on the Holy Spirit, and the use of wisdom.

Biblical Examples of Strategy

Scripture does not necessarily have to demonstrate that the Savior or the church used a strategy in their ministries or endorses in some way the use of one. This is the negative hermeneutic. Regardless, it is noteworthy that the Old and New Testaments provide us with various examples of strategy.

The Old Testament

Numerous leaders in the Old Testament ministered according to a strategy. For example, Moses was a strategic thinker. He used military strategy in most of the wars that Israel fought against its enemies (Deut. 20). Perhaps Jethro, his father-in-law, influenced him early to think and minister strategically in Exodus 18. He also used a strategy in such incidents as the spying out of Canaan in Numbers 13. Joshua also displayed his knowledge and use of military strategy in the defeat of Jericho (Josh. 6:1–6), the defeat of Ai (Josh. 8:3–23), and the defeat of the Amorites (Josh. 10:6–9). Nehemiah was a master strategist. He displayed his abilities in the rebuilding of the gates and the walls recorded in Nehemiah 3–6.

The New Testament

In the Gospels, Jesus was the master planner whose strategy was to reach out to and save all who would believe (Luke 19:10). To implement his strategy he recruited (Luke 5), discipled, and sent out (Luke 9) a motley band of men known later as his disciples or "the Twelve." He also sent out the seventy (Luke 10) as well as winning a number of other disciples among the people. Ultimately, his strategy involved a cruel death on the cross and resurrection from the dead.

The book of Acts presents a classic example of strategy in the life and ministry of the Apostle Paul. Before he ascended, the Savior provided the church with its mission or marching orders (Matt. 28:19–20; Mark 16:15). The book of Acts records how the early church understood Christ's commission, and the three missionary journeys of Paul (Acts 13:1–21:26) present the strategy they used to implement the Great Commission. Some might look to the epistles for a biblical confirmation of strategy (the negative hermeneutic). However, they contain little information on this concept. The place to look is the narrative portions of the Bible because that is where so many leaders reveal their strategies through their ministry.

Not only does much of Acts provide evidence for and information on the fact of a strategy, but the Apostle Paul, who was involved in all three missionary journeys, ministered according to a carefully developed strategy. For example, Paul did not simply wander aimlessly through an area, witnessing and ministering as he found opportunity. The evidence is that he carefully selected the cities where he might exert the greatest influence on the largest number of people. For example, why did he choose to minister and plant a church in Ephesus (Acts 19:1)? The answer is that it was a strategic city that served as a gateway to all Asia Minor. To minister in Ephesus would have a significant impact in spreading the gospel throughout Asia Minor (Acts 19:10). J. McKee Adams writes: "This selective principle is to be attributed to the guidance of the Holy Spirit. It is significant that wherever the Apostle traveled, there was a great center of cultural influence involving provincial territories. In a word, these great points, all ready at hand were converted into sources from which the Gospel was progressively heralded into all parts of contiguous regions."[4]

Questions and Strategy

Although a theology of strategy is found in the Bible, it does raise certain theological questions. For example, some would question if the concept contradicts other doctrines of the Scriptures such as the sovereignty of God, dependence on the Holy Spirit, and the use of wisdom.

Strategy and the Sovereignty of God

An important theological question is how a well-defined strategy squares with the sovereignty of God? This question surfaces the age-old tension in theology between God's sovereignty and man's free will. This issue focuses on the former. The next issue (strategy and dependence on the Holy Spirit) focuses on the latter. The question here is: Why does a ministry such as a church need a strategy when God is sovereign and will do what he pleases anyway (Acts 2:23; 4:28; Eph. 1:11)?

The answer is that in his sovereignty God has chosen to work through strategies. How else would we explain the church planting missionary journeys in Acts 13:1–21:26, and Paul's strategy of selecting not just any city but key, world-class cities of the ancient Roman Empire for church planting and evangelism?

In 1 Corinthians 3:5–7 Paul writes: "What, after all, is Apollos? And what is Paul? Only servants, through whom you came to believe—as the Lord has assigned to each his task. I planted the seed, Apollos watered it, but God made it grow. So neither he who plants nor he who waters is anything, but only God, who makes things grow." This passage shows the blend of God's sovereignty with man's responsibility. God is everything in the process of bringing people to faith. In his sovereign will, he has decided to work through people like Apollos, Paul, you, and me who function in the process as his strategic servants. One may plant the seed, another may water it, but it is God who makes it grow. I observe this truth every spring as I attempt to grow a healthy, beautiful lawn. My part is to water and fertilize my yard, but try as hard as I might, only God can make the grass grow.

Strategy and Dependence on the Holy Spirit

The other side of the theological tension between God's sovereignty and man's free will comes down on the free will side (Matt. 23:37; Luke 7:30; John 3:18). Here the question becomes: Does developing and ministering according to a strategy make us less dependent on the Holy Spirit? Are we replacing the work of the Holy Spirit in ministry with human devices and gimmicks?

The answer is that this is certainly possible. It could happen to the best of us. We must regularly depend on God and trust him for all we do in our ministries as well as our lives (Prov. 3:26). Yet God the Holy Spirit uses and works through an articulate, well-defined strategy. For example, at the very initiation of the first of what became three missionary journeys (the early church's strategy for implementing Christ's Great Commission), Luke records that the Holy Spirit was a part of the strategic process. He writes: "While they were worshipping the Lord and fasting, the Holy Spirit said, 'Set apart for me Barnabas and Saul for the work to which I have called them.' So after they had fasted and prayed, they placed their hands on them and sent them off" (Acts 13:2–3).

Strategy and Wisdom

The thrust of Scripture is that it is wise to minister according to a strategy. The term that Scripture uses is *plan*, but good plans consist of good strategies. Proverbs 16:3 reminds us of the importance of committing whatever we do to the Lord so that our plans will be congruent with his plans and succeed. What is important and encouraging in strategizing is that ultimately "the Lord works out everything for his own ends . . ." (Prov. 16:4).

Proverbs 16:9 catches both the wisdom and the balance of the human and the divine in the strategizing process: "In his heart a man plans his course, but the Lord determines his steps." Proverbs 13:16 says that a prudent man acts out of knowledge. The role of a strategy is to supply the prudent man with that knowledge. The strategy process (the internal and external audits) supplies wise leaders with the information they need to know in order to develop strategies that implement the Great Commission.

QUESTIONS FOR DISCUSSION AND REFLECTION

1. Briefly inventory your ministry and identify all the biblical functions that are present such as worship, teaching, and so on. How many did you discover? What are they? Were any prominent ones such as evangelism or teaching missing? If so, why?

2. What forms do your ministry's functions take? Have any of these forms changed in the last twenty years? The last five or ten years? How have they changed? Do you believe that this change has been good or bad? Why?

3. Identify some of your church's traditions. Which are good traditions, and which are not so good? Why? Do the members believe that any or all of these traditions are biblical? Which traditions? Is anyone trying to impose their traditions on others? If yes, what effect is this having on the ministry and its people?

4. When you examine what your church is doing, what percentage is based on Scripture? What percentage is based on culture? Give some examples. In your opinion is it acceptable to base some of what your church is doing on culture?

5. In your ministry, do people feel that they have the freedom to make changes? Can you see any areas where the church makes nonabsolutes absolutes? If yes, give some examples.

6. Give some examples where your ministry may be involved in contextualization. Give some examples where your ministry may be guilty of accommodation.

7. Have you been involved in a ministry, including your present church, that espouses and/or practices the negative hermeneutic or patternism? If yes, give some examples. What is the problem with these views?

8. Are you aware of other biblical examples of strategy that this chapter does not present? If yes, what are they? Do you believe

that we must have such examples before we are free to strategize in our ministries? If yes, what hermeneutical error might this be? What does it mean when you say that something is biblical or unbiblical?

9. How do you square the concept of strategy with God's sovereignty, dependence on the Holy Spirit, and the use of wisdom?

ENDNOTES

1. See Aubrey Malphurs, *Maximizing Your Effectiveness* (Grand Rapids, Mich.: Baker Book House, 1995), pp. 70–76.

2. Kennon Callahan, *Effective Church Leadership* (New York: Harper and Row, 1990), p. 4.

3. Francis A. Schaeffer, *The Church at the End of the 20th Century* (Wheaton, Ill.: Crossway Books, 1970), p. 68.

4. J. McKee Adams, *Biblical Backgrounds* (Nashville: Broadman Press, 1934), pp. 402–3.

PART TWO

The Process of Developing a Strategy

Strategizing is the process that determines how you will accomplish the mission of the ministry. A strategy is the product. Strategizing involves moving a person from prebirth to maturity and consists of four steps. It begins with preparation and asks: How do we prepare for the strategizing process? This is the topic of chapter 5. Next, it focuses on the person and asks: Who is our target group? This is the focus of chapter 6. Third, it moves to the program and asks: What kind of church will it take to reach our target group? This is the essence of chapter 7. It finishes with a plan and asks: How will we implement our program with our target group? This is the content of chapter 8.

CHAPTER FIVE

The Preparation for the Strategy

WORKING OFF THE SAME PAGE

"Suppose one of you wants to build a tower. Will he not first sit down and estimate the cost to see if he has enough money to complete it?"   —Luke 14:28

Finally everyone was on board or at least professed to be. The deacons of Faith Chapel Church had debated the issue until late into the night. Pastor Robert Smith, however, was determined that they begin to rethink their strategy as a church. Much of the opposition came from his head deacon. Smith was not convinced that the man understood the difference between a strategy and marketing. However, that did not seem to matter. They met on a number of occasions for breakfast, and Pastor Robert gradually won the man over to his view. He believes that the deciding moment was when he appealed to the man to reach out to the younger families who had left the church. The head deacon's son was one of those who had dropped out of church, vowing never to return. Pastor Robert had asked the deacon a penetrating question: What would you be willing to change if it meant reinteresting your son and his family and others like him in spiritual things and the church?

Now the question becomes: What is the next step? Having gained board approval, where does Pastor Robert go from here? The answer is preparation. On the one hand, part 1 (chaps. 1–4) has provided us with a broad preparation for developing a strategy. It has presented the general issues one must think through before even attempting to develop a strategy. In part 2, we move into the specific, actual "hands on" preparation necessary to start the strategy development process. The ministry team will need to think through at least six issues as it prepares itself to develop a strategy or redevelop its strategy for effective ministry in the twenty-first century. These issues are need, readiness, personnel, time, cost, and place.

Before we look at each issue, I want to provide a warning and present an assumption. As you begin to work with and through the strategizing process, I must warn you that there will be times when you will be tempted to distort the information you uncover, especially that which relates to your success or lack thereof in ministry. There is, therefore, a critical need for pursuing the truth and operating with candor, openness, and accuracy throughout the process. Otherwise the findings will be skewed and not only misleading but worthless to your ministry.

This chapter does not say a lot about prayer and trusting God for the ministry. This is because I assume the importance of both. The need for a leader to bathe the process in prayer and trust God every step of the way is essential and vital to the ministry's success (Prov. 14:12; 16:3).

THE NEED FOR A STRATEGY

One of the first questions a ministry must ask as it prepares to develop a strategy or redevelop its strategy is this: Is the organization ready to begin this process? If the leaders of a ministry or the people who make up the organization are not convinced that there exists a need for a strategy or a new strategy, then either nothing will happen, or they will approach the process with little enthusiasm. Consequently, the key people in the organization must both see and own the need for having a strategy from the beginning of the process.

The important questions are: What can we do to help them see the need? and How do you convince them of such a need? One answer is to present the information found in chapter 1 of this book. Ask each leader to read through it and answer the questions at the end. That alone, however, will not be enough. The rest of the answer is to follow up that information by performing an internal evaluation of the church or parachurch organization. The internal evaluation consists of a series of audits and critical questions that help everyone to understand how the ministry is doing in several key areas. I would suggest that you as the leader first work through the questions on your own. Then you will need to walk your leadership through the same questions.

The Ministry Audit

The ministry audit attempts to assess the ministry's strengths, limitations, and weaknesses. It is important that you be objective in this process. Therefore, not only should you attempt to answer them yourself, but you should also ask other interested people as well. If your ministry is a church, then quiz the staff, board, attendees, visitors, and so on. Also consider asking trusted people in the community who are not a part of your ministry.

Strengths

Answer the following questions about your strengths or core competencies (what you're good at) as a ministry:

- What are your strengths as a church?
- Do you have any distinctive, unique competencies?
- What quality or attribute of the ministry sets it off from the other ministries in your area? What do you provide that others do not?
- What are you good at? What do you do well?
- Name your top three strengths.

Identifying your core competencies will help you to focus your energies and resources as a ministry.

Limitations

No church can do everything well. That is an impossibility. It is comparable to a skilled basketball player attempting to play football or a huge defensive tackle in football trying to become a professional ice skater. A genuinely helpful audit should also identify limitations as well. Answer the following questions about your limitations as a ministry:

- What can you not do well? What should you not attempt?
- What do others provide that it is not possible for you to provide currently?
- What do others provide that you might never be able to provide due to your ministry area (inner-city, suburbs, rural area) or ministry target (unreached people groups)?

Weaknesses

Your weaknesses are those areas where you have some abilities but for some reason are not doing them well. If something is worth doing, then it is worth doing well or do not even attempt it. The Bible encourages us to do our work "as unto the Lord" (Eph. 6:5–8; Col. 3:23–24). Answer the following questions about your weaknesses:

- What can you accomplish well that you are doing only average or poorly?
- Name your top three weaknesses.
- What other corrections do you need to make?

The Life-cycle Audit

Like people, every ministry has a life cycle (fig. 5.1). At some point, the church is planted and begins its life. In most cases the new church grows, but eventually it will plateau. Unless the church makes some changes, in time it starts to decline. If that decline is not interrupted, then it will eventually die. The performance audit assesses where your church is on the ministry life cycle. Answer the following questions:

- Is your ministry growing? Do you know why? What can you do to keep it growing?
- Has your ministry plateaued? Do you know why? What will you do to help it grow again?
- Is your ministry in decline? Do you know why? What will you do to turn this around?
- Is your ministry over? Is it time to shut the ministry down, and begin somewhere else?

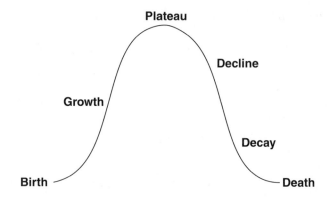

Figure 5.1 Church Life Cycles

The Mission Audit

Every ministry must have a mission if it is to succeed. The mission is what the ministry is attempting to accomplish; it is what the ministry is all about. The mission audit attempts to help the ministry to determine how well it is accomplishing its mission. Answer the following questions about your ministry's mission:

- Does you ministry have a mission statement? What is it?
- Has your ministry clearly articulated that mission statement? How does it communicate that statement to those in the ministry?
- How well is the ministry accomplishing the mission statement?
- Where are you now in relation to where you want to be or should be?
- If there is a gap, how great a gap is it? What will it take to bridge the gap? (Remember: The greater the gap the more the change!)

The Energy Audit

A ministry's energy has to do with the degree of effort or intensity that it exerts in pursuit of its mission and all its various activities. A ministry that is growing and accomplishing well its mission will have a high degree of energy as people will pursue their ministries with much enthusiasm. A ministry that is on its last leg will display little, if any, energy at all. An energy audit seeks to determine the state or level of the energy in your ministry. Answer the following questions about your ministry's energy level:

- Is the level of energy in your church high? How do you know? How do you explain this?
- Is the level of energy in your church low to nonexistent? Why? What does this tell you about your church?
- Is the energy level somewhere between high and low? Where would you place it? Is this good or bad?
- Is your energy level going down or up? Why? If it is going down, what does this mean?

The Emotions Audit

Since every ministry consists of people, corporately it will reflect the characteristics of its individuals. One characteristic is their emotional state. Their emotions will be either high, low, or somewhere in between.

When a ministry is strong, it will be high emotionally. When it is not strong, it will be low emotionally.

- As a whole where are your people emotionally?
- What adjectives would you use to describe the emotional state of your ministry (upbeat, excited, downbeat, struggling, tired)?
- How will this affect the organization's capacity to move in a strategic direction?

Besides the ministry audits above, the internal evaluation consists of several critical questions about your ministry. These will also aid you in determining the need for developing a strategy.

Ministry Threats

Every ministry needs to regularly consider activities and events that threaten its very existence much less its ability to accomplish its mission.

The question here is: What are the immediate and long-term threats to your ministry? Review the following list of threats and determine if any are relevant to your ministry situation:

- Expanding inner city and a changing, dying community
- Growing area crime rate
- Saturation or proliferation of similar churches in the area
- Congregational aging (the majority of your people are over 65)
- Few, if any, people joining the church
- Few young people (Boomers, Busters, and so on) in the church
- Youth leaving church when they complete high school
- A significant number of attendees and members no longer living in the church's community
- Businesses moving out of the area, leaving numerous abandoned buildings

What other threats are there to your ministry that are not mentioned in the above list?

Other Ministries

It is most helpful when evaluating your ministry, to look at other similar ministries in the area. How they are doing and what they are doing can help promote the effectiveness of your ministry. Consider the following questions:

- Identify some of the other ministries in your community. Are they churches or parachurch organizations? How are they doing?
- Do you and/or your people view them as ministry competitors or companions?
- How are you like them? How are you different from them?
- What are their strengths, limitations, and weaknesses?
- What are their visions, values, strategies?
- How do you stack up with them?

Ministry Competitors

Whether we like it or not, there are other organizations or events in our communities that compete with us for the attention of people, whether they are our present members or potential members. Review the following to identify some of your competitors:

- Other churches or parachurch organizations; other religious organizations or cult ministries
- The entertainment industry (movies, television, and so on)
- Athletics: participative sports such as softball, bowling leagues, and so on; viewer sports such as professional or college football, baseball, basketball, and so on
- Health clubs and fitness centers
- Leisure activities: reading, writing, and so on
- Recreation: lakes, ocean, mountains, and others
- Marketplace: shopping malls, department stores, and so on
- Family time

Can you identify any other ministry competitors?

Ministry Opportunities

Not only will there be ministry threats and competitors in one's community, but there will be numerous opportunities for ministry. However, churches do not always have eyes to see these opportunities. When there are problems, the church will often turn its focus inwardly, on itself. Review the following list to determine some of the ministry opportunities in your target area:

- Unreached people in the community
- New people moving into the area
- New or old unreached people groups in area

- Nearby elementary schools, high schools, colleges, and universities
- International students at the above schools
- Nearby armed services facilities (Army, Navy, Air Force, Coast Guard, Marines)
- Singles, and single parents
- Those with emotional problems (twelve-step programs, Al-Anon, and so on)
- Senior citizens
- Street people

Can you think of any ministry opportunities not mentioned above?

Ministry Resources

Every church exists to accomplish ministry. However, its ability to accomplish its ministries depends on its resources. What resources are available to your ministry and how strong are they? Examine and rate the following resources:

- Finances
- People
- Property
- Facilities

THE READINESS FOR A STRATEGY

If there was any question of the need for a strategy, then the preceding section should have surfaced a number of issues requiring a strategic approach. Assuming that need, the next question in this section is: Is the organization ready for a strategy? That a ministry or church needs a strategy does not necessarily mean that it is ready to develop one. For example, a child may be at a point of intellectual development when he or she should be ready to learn how to read. He or she has begun school, and the class is at a point where the teacher is ready to provide instruction about reading and see that each student develops strong reading skills. However, if the child is not ready or able to learn, then even the most competent reading specialist may not succeed.

If a church, including the pastor and/or board, is not ready, then the strategizing process will not happen, and even the best possible strategy will not work. To attempt to design and implement a strategy with a ministry that either does not see the need or is not ready is like trying to teach a child to read who is not ready. And should it happen, the process will not only be a waste of time and energy, but it will discourage anyone from ever attempting it again.

One key to an organization's readiness to develop a strategy is its openness to change. Developing or redeveloping a strategy means that the ministry must make some changes. In many ministries at the end of the twentieth century, there is a need for a great deal of change. A specific ministry's willingness to make at least some, if not all, the changes necessary reflects its state of change readiness. But how can you know? The only way you can assess a readiness for change is to ask questions. I have provided a *Readiness for Change Inventory* in the appendixes to help you with this process. You may want to use the inventory as a review of your ministry or use it to surface the kinds of questions you need to ask in the assessment process.

Another key to a church's readiness for a strategy is its pastor. If the pastor sees the need and is ready to develop a strategy, it might happen. Much depends, however, on his age, tenure at the church, leadership abilities, knowledge of the change process, and credibility with the congregation. If he does not favor the development of or a redevelopment of a strategy, it is unlikely to happen because he is the one who needs to lead the church in the development of its strategy.

A pastor might oppose a change in strategy for various reasons. He may be a person for whom change is not easy. There are some temperaments that are change resistant.[1] He could be an older person who is close to retirement and prefers not to start something he cannot finish. He has wisely decided to leave any changes to his successor. He could be a leader who is locked into an old-paradigm mind-set and does not see the need for any new-paradigm strategies. He is convinced that the old paradigm is sufficient to accomplish the mission. He believes that the solution is to work harder, to redouble all efforts at the old strategy. If this person can't change, then there's not a lot of hope for his future.

A third key to a church's readiness to develop a strategy is its board. If the leadership board wants it to happen, then most likely it will. If they are for it and the pastor is against it, then they may replace him or wait until he retires. However, if the leadership of the church or ministry does not support strategy development, then it is not likely to occur. If the pastor is for it, they will simply drag their heels, argue with him, and fail to act. Somehow he must convince them of the need and help them to change their minds, or he will have to give up on the idea or postpone it.

It is important that a leadership board understands its purpose or function as a board. Most boards consist of laypeople who need good training. Unfortunately, most board members tend to feel that their job is to maintain unity and keep the peace. After all, if there is an explosive confrontation and people leave the church, then the finances will evaporate and the ministry could die. No board wants that on its conscience. Consequently, if a few people complain, especially older people with deep pockets, the board listens and tends to give in to their demands. The result is that a few people exert their will over the majority.

If a church expects to develop a strategy to accomplish its mission, then it will need to deal with its "squeaky wheels." The board, along with the pastor, will have to exert some leadership. This means making what, for some, will be unpopular decisions. They must deal with and challenge the resistors. They must stand up for what they know is correct even if it threatens the very existence of the church. It would be better for the church to close its doors than to continue without either a mission or a strategy to accomplish that mission. I would question if a church without a mission and/or a strategy is, in fact, a church.

Here are some questions that, along with the *Readiness for Change Inventory* in the appendixes, will help you to determine your church's readiness for change.

- Is the pastor ready to develop a strategy? Is he convinced of the need for a strategy? Has he internalized the concept emotionally? Does he model it? How about his staff? How about the lay leaders and workers?
- Is the board ready to develop a strategy? Are they or key members of the board convinced of the need for a strategy or a new strategy?
- Is the congregation ready to be a part of a new strategy? Who is and who is not?
- Where might you anticipate some resistance? What is it and how strong is it? How do you plan to deal with it if you are to move forward?
- What will it take to get everyone on board? Is the any need for retooling?

THE PERSONNEL FOR A STRATEGY

When a ministry such as a church decides to develop or retool its strategy, it has to make a number of vital decisions. Perhaps one of the most important is: Who crafts the strategy as the church's strategy personnel?

The answer to that question and the ultimate responsibility rests with the leadership. The leadership, especially the senior pastor or point leader on the team, is responsible to develop the ministry strategy. That is one reason why it is so important that he sees the need for and wants to craft a carefully thought through, well-developed strategy. If he does not, then there will always be some excuse why he has not gotten around to it.

Strategy development is more a function of management than leadership. Consequently, those with leadership gifts and no management abilities may find it difficult to focus on strategy development. However, as leaders they should see the need for and importance of the strategy to the ministry and do whatever it takes to get the job done.

I would assign the responsibility for the initial development of the strategy to the senior pastor of a larger church or the sole pastor of a smaller church. As the leader, he is responsible for initiating and coming up with the rough draft. Should he find this difficult, then he can turn to a book such as this one or a consultant for help in the process.

The strategy, however, is not to be the product of the pastor alone, but of all who are involved in the ministry. The initial document is his, but others must get their fingerprints on the strategy, or they will never take ownership of it. "Others" includes the board and/or other key leaders in the ministry. The pastor should submit his product to the church board for their input. The quality of their contribution depends on the quality of the board. A good board will make a strong contribution, even if it is simply recognizing a good document and not attempting to add anything to it. They will know a good strategy from a poor one. A poor or nominal board will have little to contribute or may even attempt to derail the process.

Next, other ministry leaders such as board chairpersons and even small-group leaders need to see and interact with the strategy statement. These people often provide helpful input. They see things from a different perspective than the pastor and board. They bring insight to the strategy from the perspective of their individual ministries and the people who are a part of their ministries. If possible it needs to be a "grass roots" or "bottom-up" process involving those who will be affected by or implementing the strategy.

The size of the governing structure will ultimately dictate who reviews and is involved in the development of the strategy. In a large church, it would not be possible for everyone to provide feedback. Consequently, the statement would be the creation of the pastor, his staff, and the board.

In a small church, it might be possible for the entire congregation to participate.

The strategy development process may exclude the squeaky wheels. Most leaders know who they are. The wise leader or pastor will listen to the squeaky wheels of the ministry but not let them influence the entire church. It is important to the health of the ministry that the squeaky wheels not drive the wagon!

Having worked as a consultant, I would highly recommend that you use one in the crafting of your ministry strategy. A consultant usually proves worth his or her weight in gold for several reasons. First, a consultant informs the ministry and helps those involved to understand the entire process. A good one has been through the process and knows where the difficulties lie. Second, that he or she is an outsider satisfies the group's need for objectivity. Third, a consultant lends credibility to the pastor or point leader and the whole idea of the process. This is what I commonly refer to as "the prophet is without honor" syndrome. For some reason most churches grant more credibility to a consultant who comes in from outside a ministry than the people such as the pastor who are already a part of the ministry.

Some ministries find it valuable to use an ad hoc planning team or strategic ministry team to develop and then oversee the implementation of the ministry strategy. They would be a group of five to eight people, including the pastor, who have a strong interest in and growing expertise in strategy development. Since the strategizing process is ongoing, they might become responsible for researching the community and keeping the strategy on the cutting edge of the community. Some might serve as trend spotters: to scan, clip, and review interesting articles on future area trends from newspapers, periodicals, and other sources.

THE TIME FOR A STRATEGY

A characteristic of most people at the end of the twentieth century and the beginning of the twenty-first century is busyness. In short, most do not have much discretionary time. Consequently, a necessary question in preparation for developing a strategy is: How long will the crafting process take? Initially, it will take ten to twenty full days. This time, however, consists of one- to three-hour meetings along with a few half-day and full-day meetings spread over a period of several months. Remember, it always takes longer than anyone anticipates. Once you begin, however, you never stop the process. You must view it as an ongoing ministry to the church, not an event. Once you have developed the document, you must regularly conduct external audits of the community and internal audits of the church or risk losing contact with the community and your ministry.

Several factors affect the time that it takes to craft a significant strategy. First, is everyone on board? If not, then it will take much longer to develop a strategy—if it happens at all. You should expect some conflict, clashes, and disagreements. While they are an inevitable part of the process, they will add time to it. Another factor is the availability of the necessary data that go into the strategy. For example, it may take some time to collect the information that goes into an external or internal audit. Not every ministry has access to demographic information on the community, especially countries outside North America.

THE COST OF A STRATEGY

The two most frequently asked questions by people on a committee or planning team are invariably the same: What are the time commitments? and How much will it cost? People tend to ask about time commitments first since most people already have crammed schedules. Our time is more valuable to us than our money. The money question, however, is just as important. In Luke 14:28–33 Jesus taught that it is crucial to estimate the cost of a project before commencing that project. Consequently, we must ask: How much will it cost to craft a tailor-made strategy for our church or ministry?

Several costs may be involved. First, it will cost you and your team a considerable amount of time. While I have covered the time aspects above, here time will also mean money because the church will be paying its staff for their involvement, and laypeople may be missing out on pay because they've taken time off from work. However, this is to be expected because strategizing must be viewed as a regular, critical component of any ministry that has a mission. As long as a church or parachurch ministry has a clear, concise mission statement, it must regularly evaluate and retool its strategy. This is because to a certain extent a strategy is based on factors and conditions in the community. When the community changes, that in turn affects the ministry.

In the last section of this chapter, I will recommend that the strategy personnel attempt to get away to prepare the strategy. There are many advantages to meeting away from the church or ministry facilities. Using a retreat facility will probably cost the ministry some use fee, depending on how elaborate those facilities are.

I have suggested above that it is wise to use a consultant in the strategy preparation process. Some denominations have these people on staff and may provide their services at little or no cost to their member churches. However, most do charge for their services. In my experience, the average fee ranges from $500 to $1,200 a day. In most cases, the better consultants merit the higher fee. The problem is that most ministries feel that they cannot afford this kind of counsel and assistance, especially smaller churches. As a consultant, I view it from a different perspective. I am convinced that a ministry cannot afford to engage in the process without a good consultant. A consultant's knowledge and expertise usually make the difference between a well-designed strategy and a poorly designed one.

Finally, a good strategy will use demographic and psychographic materials. Demographics tell you who the people are who live in your ministry community—their age, size of family, kind of residence, education, occupation, marital status, income, and much more. Psychographics provide you with information on these people's needs, hopes, dream, aspirations, and so on. Both are vital to developing a good strategy. I will say more about them in the next chapter.

Some denominational agencies also provide this information for their member churches at little or no cost. However, most ministries will need to purchase this information. The good news is that the cost of the information you need is reasonable. The companies that provide demographic and psychographic material offer various packages of information at differing costs. Regardless, most charge from $200 to $500 for their research and services. I would suggest that you contact an organization such as Church Information and Development Services (CIDS) for cost information.[2]

THE PLACE FOR A STRATEGY

The crafting of a significant strategy to accomplish the ministry's mission requires time as stated above. Sometimes it consists of what I refer to as "snatches of time." By this, I mean an hour here and one half hour there. However, to plan well, the ministry team will need to set aside several days for maximum production.

Many teams use their own facilities for these longer planning periods. I would suggest that the team consider using a retreat center or some other place that is geographically removed enough to eliminate interruptions. There is good precedent for this approach. In Mark 1:35, the Savior left the house where he was staying and went to a solitary place for prayer. He needed to be alone to worship his Father without any interruptions. Since the planning and strategizing retreat will involve some worship and the need to be free from interruptions, we would be wise to follow the Savior's example.

The strategy personnel need a place that provides them with maximum opportunity to work creatively. A strategy is wrapped in the foil of creativity and baked in the oven of time. Interruptions can prove disastrous to the creative processes. Therefore, I would encourage any strategizing team to get away geographically as well as emotionally when using larger chunks of time such as a day or more.

Numerous locations are available for such a retreat. The first location that I would pursue is one that belongs to an individual who is identified in some way with the ministry. For example, a member of your church may own a lake house or a weekend cabin in the mountains. Most likely, they will let the team use the facilities for little or no cost. Other good locations are a hotel or motel meeting room, a retreat conference center, a private club, lake house, ski lodge, or large private home. Some churches in Texas will often retreat to one of the many ranch houses that dot the Texas landscape. An option for a parachurch ministry but not a church is to use its ministry facilities during non-business hours such as a weekend. However, most teams seem to accomplish more when they utilize other locations.

A wise choice is to find a place that is not so far from home that the strategy personnel cannot return there after the meetings are over for the day. There are advantages to sleeping in your own bed at night and being with your family. If the group opts to spend the night, then make sure the facility is adequate so that all involved have comfortable sleeping accommodations. People do not last long or function well when they miss sleep and their families.

QUESTIONS FOR DISCUSSION AND REFLECTION

1. Is your church or ministry ready to develop or retool its strategy? What might you do to help your people see the need? Based on a ministry audit, what are your strengths, limitations, and weaknesses? Did you question anyone outside your ministry? If not, why not?

2. According to your performance audit, is your ministry growing, plateaued, or in decline? Do you know why? If your ministry is plateaued or in decline, what do you plan to do about it?

3. Does your ministry have a mission statement? If yes, how well is

it accomplishing the mission? If it does not have a mission statement, do you plan to develop one? What did you learn about your ministry based on the Mission Audit?

4. Is the energy level in your church high, low, or somewhere in between? Is this good or bad? What do you plan to do about it? What have you learned about your ministry based on the Energy Audit?

5. Are the emotions of your people high, low, or in between? How important is this emotional level to the ministry? How does it work for and against a ministry? What else have you learned from the Emotions Audit?

6. What are the various threats to your ministry, and what do you plan to do about them? What other ministries are in your community, and what can you learn from them? Who are your ministry competitors, and how have they affected your ministry? What are your ministry opportunities, and what do you plan to do about them? What ministry resources do you have, and what do you need?

7. How open is your church or ministry to change? Does the pastor see the need for a strategy or a new strategy? The board? If either the pastor or board is against developing a strategy for the church, how will this affect the chances for a new strategy for your ministry? Does your church have any squeaky wheels? If yes, are the squeaky wheels against developing a strategy? Are the squeaky wheels driving the wagon?

8. Who are or should be the strategy personnel in your ministry? Has the pastor or point person taken responsibility for the strategy? If yes, is he doing it alone, or is he involving other significant people in the process? Have you thought about using a consultant to help you in crafting your strategy? Why or why not? Is cost a factor?

9. How much time should you allow for the strategy development process? Is this realistic? Have you considered all the various factors? What do you think it will cost to develop a strategy? Where will you get the money? Where will you meet while you work on the strategy? How does the team feel about meeting in this place?

ENDNOTES

1. See chapter 6 in my book *Pouring New Wine into Old Wineskins: How to Change a Church Without Destroying It* (Grand Rapids, Mich.: Baker Book House, 1994).

2. The address for Church Information and Development Services (CIDS) is 3001 Redhill Avenue, Suite 2-220, Costa Mesa, CA 92626-9664 (800-442-6277).

CHAPTER SIX

The Person of the Strategy

IDENTIFYING YOUR CUSTOMER

"For the Son of Man came to seek and to save what was lost."
—Luke 19:10

"For God, who was at work in the ministry of Peter as an apostle to the Jews, was also at work in my ministry as an apostle to the Gentiles."
—Galatians 2:8

Pastor Robert Smith worked hard at preparing his team for the development of a new church strategy. According to his final tally, all on his board understood the need and were ready for a new strategy. It was a matter of opening their eyes to see and acknowledge what everyone secretly knew in his or her heart but had difficulty admitting—Faith Chapel Church was dying. The death would not happen overnight. It was a slow and painful event that was destined to occur unless they did something soon. As one elderly board member admitted, "When I look out across our congregation, I don't see many young faces. All I see are a bunch of wonderful, old people. When they're gone, we're gone. We've got to do something!"

The board had decided that they would be the strategy personnel to craft the new strategy and that Pastor Smith would be the point man on their team. Already he was busy developing a blueprint or document that would consist of both a mission statement and a strategy. Faith Chapel had never articulated its mission as a church. Consequently, no one was sure of its direction. And the development of a strategy assumes the existence of a mission or clear direction.

Pastor Robert's job would be to bring the finished document

consisting of a mission statement and a strategy back to them for their input. They anticipated that it would take them about six months before the final product would be ready, and they decided to invite some guest speakers to free up some of the pastor's time to work on the document. One of the board members with deep pockets had volunteered to underwrite the entire project that included the following: a board retreat at a cattle ranch turned conference center, the services of a consultant, and a detailed demographic and psychographic study of their community.

The development of a mission statement for Faith Chapel Church was no mystery. It was easy; it would be the Great Commission. Pastor Robert had studied it in his classes at seminary, but now he understood its importance to his ministry. One of his professors had also lectured on strategy development. Pastor Robert dug up his yellowed class notes and blew the dust off them. As he reviewed them, he discovered that having prepared his people to develop the strategy, his next step was to determine their target group.

In trying to preach the gospel, most churches attempt a broad, unfocused approach, or what I call the "shotgun method." They hope to reach anybody and everybody. While that is a noble goal, the reality is that they will not and cannot attain it. Instead, most who attempt the shotgun method end up reaching no one in particular. That is why it takes all kinds of churches to reach all kinds of people. Therefore, it is strategic to take a more focused approach or what I call the "rifle method." This involves targeting a specific group or groups of people, as did Paul, who targeted Gentiles, and Peter, who targeted Jews.

There are four steps in determining the target group. First, you must identify your specific target group—who are they? Next, you must locate them—where are they? Third, you will gather information about them— what are their needs, hopes, hurts, and aspirations? Finally, you will construct an individual profile that will help your people to identify and remember the group.

Work through the following material and answer as many questions about your target group as possible. Do not rush. Give yourself enough time to do accurate work. You may have to do some research at a nearby library, consult with a company specializing in demographics, or interview someone from your target area. Regardless, the accuracy of the information is critical to the entire process.

IDENTIFY THE TARGET GROUP

An important principle that every person in Christian service must remember is that ministry is about people. We are in the people business! People, both saved and lost, are important to God (Luke 5:27–32; 15:1–32; 19:1–10; Mark 9:33–37). The Father gave his Son for people (John 3:16). The Son gave his life for people, even his enemies (Rom. 5:8). Paul was willing to give up his salvation (if that were possible) for Jewish people (Rom. 9:1–3). If people matter to God, then they should matter to us. Our ministries need to be vision-focused, values-driven, and people-centered as opposed to program-centered. The unfortunate reality is that many pastors like to teach people; the verdict is still out, however, as to whether they actually like people!

Since ministry is all about people, it is imperative that you answer these critical questions: Who is our actual target person? and Whom are you trying to reach? Other equally important questions are: Who *should be* our target person? Who are you not targeting that you should be reaching? and Who is your *potential* target person? These are the critical questions in this section. However, you must make some theological and philosophical decisions before and as you answer these questions.

Will You Target Lost or Saved People?

Some churches target the lost person. This is highly commendable in that people are being saved and passing from the kingdom of darkness into the kingdom of light (Col. 1:12–13). The problem is that new Christians in an evangelism-only ministry tend to dry up spiritually and blow away to other ministries that provide more nurture and teaching. Another option is to stay and embrace superficiality. The Great Commission includes more than just bringing people into the kingdom, as important as that is.

Most churches, by happenstance or by design, target saved people. Many churches are too dependent on attracting new members who have become dissatisfied with their present churches. This approach, however, attracts disgruntled people who bring all their problems and dissatisfactions to the new church. Some churches that focus almost exclusively on Bible exposition by a popular teaching pastor fall under this category. These teaching churches grow more by transfer and biological growth than by conversion growth. Other churches in the area often accuse such churches of "stealing" their members. The problem with this approach is that the church is supposed to be reaching lost people as well as teaching believers (Mark 16:15).

The Great Commission addresses the needs of both the lost and the saved. It begins with lost people (Luke 5, 15, 19). Christ did not come to reach the righteous but sinners! It also involves, however, edification or nurture as well as salvation. Believers must grow in their faith and become more Christlike. Consequently, the strategy needs to move people from spiritual prebirth to maturity. It must accept them wherever they are in their spiritual journey and make them completely committed disciples. The Great Commission begins with a pagan, totally consumed with himself or herself, and moves that person to a completely committed Christian, totally consumed with Christ.

Will You Target Churched or Unchurched People?

While churches may assume that they are reaching the unchurched, the reality is that their programs are targeted to attract those already churched. To target churched people is to leave your ministry open and vulnerable to the accusation of "sheep stealing" as mentioned above. Some Bible-teaching churches are doing this and are not even aware of it. An alternative exists. Approximately 80 percent of Americans are unchurched. Most of that 80 percent live in Washington State, Oregon, and Nevada, but many are also in the Northeast, and there is a growing number in the South. There are two types of unchurched people. One type is the unchurched, unsaved. They are the people described in Matthew 13:19, and we must target them (Luke 19:1–10). Another is the unchurched saved. They are often, but not always, believers who fade in the stretch (Matt. 13:20–21). Here the church's job is to attract them back to itself, but not to the 1940s and 1950s paradigms that so many, especially the Baby Boomers and Busters, have walked away from.

Will You Target Seekers?

Seekers are spiritually receptive people. They are lost individuals who through the convicting work of the Holy Spirit are interested in spiritual truth and want to know more (John 16:8–11). They are not far from the Savior. Biblical examples are Zacchaeus in Luke 15, Nicodemus in John 3:1–21, the Ethiopian eunuch in Acts 8:26, and Cornelius in Acts 10. They may hear the word but do not understand it, and Satan comes and snatches it away (Matt. 13:19). Many adults from the baby boom and baby bust generations are seekers. A large number of them are interested in spiritual truth, but they are not looking for it in the typical established church of the past. On the basis of their receptivity and responsiveness it makes sense that we target those who are interested in spiritual truth and are close to faith.

However, churches consciously or unconsciously approach seekers in various ways—some good and some not so good. I separate these approaches into four categories.

The Seeker-Driven Church

All aspects of the seeker-driven ministry are designed with the seeker in mind, especially the sermons, meeting times, design of the services, and more. The Christians in these churches want to reach their lost friends to the extent that they are willing to set aside some of their expectations and preferences. Most often there is a special service for unbelievers and a separate service for believers. This is because many seeker-driven churches design their Sunday morning services to supplement the evangelistic efforts of their members who have discovered that their lost friends will come to church only on Sunday mornings. The believers' worship service takes place sometime during the week. Willow Creek Community Church in Barrington, Illinois, has popularized this model and has used this approach to reach numerous lost people for the Savior.

One disadvantage of the seeker-driven approach in smaller churches is that the believers may go spiritually undernourished. The seeker-sensitive model is labor-intensive, and the smaller church may not have enough personnel to accomplish all the needed tasks. Non-Christians can be very critical and expect churches to do everything well. Consequently, the pastor pours much of his time into the weekend seeker service. The result is that often he has very little time and energy for a midweek believers' service. Church workers are affected as well. Thus, he provides little for Christians, who tend to drift away to other ministries that will help them move toward spiritual maturity.

The Seeker-Friendly Church

The seeker-friendly ministry is carefully designed with both the seeker and the believer in mind. Usually there are no separate services for the believer and unbeliever. Both groups are present at a Sunday morning service that attempts to reach them together. Sermons are topical, relevant, and biblical. Pastors design their messages to have an impact on both groups. The services are usually contemporary, upbeat, and celebrative.

The church encourages its people to bring their lost friends to the weekend service. They provide much more for lost people than just a gospel presentation tacked on to the end of a sermon directed primarily to Christians. The worship focuses on believers but is done in such a way that lost people understand what is taking place. The idea is to replicate 1 Corinthians 14:24–25: the unbeliever walks into the service, is convicted of his or her sin, and worships God, "exclaiming that God is really with you."

The Seeker-Tolerant Church

Seeker-tolerant churches are contemporary churches that focus on Christians. In many ways, they are like the typical traditional churches of the 1930s through the 1950s, only they have adopted a more contemporary, relevant style. They give lip service to evangelism but have not factored it into their programs. Many are contemporary teaching churches that tend to emphasize the cognitive more than the emotive or applicational side of people. A number also provide small group ministries in an attempt to help their members establish and build authentic biblical community. However, because of their contemporary format and small-group opportunities (especially those designed to help people with addictions), they may attract and win seekers anyway, leaving the impression that they are more evangelistic than they really are.

The Seeker-Hostile Church

These are older, established traditional churches that knowingly or unknowingly minister only to believers. Faith Chapel Church is a seeker-hostile church but does not realize it. The attitude of many of the saints toward the lost is that they are welcome but on our terms. Sermons are characterized by "insider talk" or "temple-talk." For example, they use terms that unbelievers do not understand such as *propitiation, redemption, reconciliation, benediction, manse, narthex,* and *vestibule.* Some of these are biblical terms. However, leaders must realize that they were common terms used in the first-century culture as well as in the Scriptures. Lost people in the first century would have understood them. Not only do lost people not understand them today, but I am convinced that not many Christians understand them either.

The program of the seeker-hostile church reflects life and worship as it was in the 1940s and 1950s. During the worship service, they may ask visitors to stand, be recognized, and tell a little about themselves. They may ask them to wear a large visitor ribbon or button so people will recognize and welcome them. While their intentions are good, these churches must realize that many lost people who are visiting want to remain anonymous. They are simply checking out the church or visiting incognito to see if they can find God there. If they cannot, then they want to quietly and unobtrusively move on to another church in their search for God. The service itself may be long, often makes a strong appeal for money, and finishes with an extended altar call. Today's seeker finds this a strange and alienating experience.

To target unchurched seekers, however, means that you will have to create an environment that does not unnecessarily or needlessly run them off. That does not mean that you will avoid preaching and teaching the whole counsel of God (Acts 20:27). Remember, they are interested in spiritual truth. In Acts 2, Peter went so far as to tell around three thousand Jews that they were responsible for Christ's death! But there is a way in which you do this. I believe that Peter spoke out of a deep, compassionate, authentic love for these people. He really cared about them, and I believe that they knew it. You would be surprised what people, even lost people, will do when they know someone authentically cares about them.

Will You Target People Like Us?

While we must be willing to reach anybody and everybody, the reality is that we cannot and will not reach everybody. When you try to reach everyone in general (the shotgun method), you reach no one in particular, and few are happy. It is like trying to sell Corvettes to everyone, including young couples with several small kids. They are in the market for a family car, not a sports car. While everyone seems to need a car, not everyone needs or wants the same kind of car.

That the people we are trying to reach are unbelievers with different cultural tastes in what is now a multicultural America makes it difficult to get everyone together in the same church. People resist being assimilated into the dominant culture, whether society in general or the church, believing that there is nothing wrong with their ethnicity or their own culture. Scripture would seem to agree. For example, at Pentecost each nation heard the gospel in its own tongue, implying that every tongue is a worthy vehicle of the gospel. In Acts 15, the decision of the Jerusalem Council was that the Gentiles did not have to become cultural Jews to be saved. No theologically correct culture exists. The Bible does not promote one culture over another. Also, people feel an affinity with those who are most like them and understand them and their culture best, and they desire that other cultures recognize and respect them. Where this is problematic and wrong biblically is when we are not open to accepting and reaching other people because of their race, color, gender, or income, and thus discriminate against them.

The truth is that no church can be culturally neutral, and every church reflects to a great degree the culture of its people. Different cultures worship God in different ways: Their music is different, their preaching style is different, they even take an offering differently. Nothing is wrong with this as long as these practices do not contradict Scripture or discriminate in any way against people. I am convinced that God gives the church much freedom in this area.[1] However, some churches convince themselves that their way (their tradition) is the only way to worship and serve God and are guilty of cultural elitism. Again, the Jerusalem Council in Acts 15 decided that one does not have to adopt a different culture to be saved.

The early church solved the problem of differences by target grouping. For instance, Paul, a Jew, with a cross-cultural gift (Eph. 3:7–8), pursued unreached Gentiles in areas where others had not ministered and Christ was not known (Gal. 2:7; Rom. 15:20; 2 Cor. 10:15–16). Peter, who was a Jew, targeted the Jews (Gal. 2:7). Certain New Testament books target particular people and groups. The gospel of Matthew targeted Jews, Mark's gospel targeted Gentiles in general and Romans in particular, and Luke focused on Gentiles.

On the one hand, churches must be ready and willing to minister the gospel to anyone (Eph. 3:1–13). On the other hand, they must ask: Who realistically can we reach? Who will respond to us? The answer initially is: people who are most like you, people who feel an affinity with you. People operate along lines of affinity. This may involve family and friends. Jesus encouraged the man healed of demon-possession to return to his family and village rather than accompany him in his ministry (Mark 5:18–20). That is why Andrew, after he met Jesus, went and found Simon, and Philip found Nathaniel (John 1:43–45). Affinity may also involve ethnicity. The Samaritan woman instinctively went back to her fellow Samaritans with her story about Christ (John 4:28–30). This is most natural and seems to be a theme in the gospel of John.

Over the past years, Dallas, Texas, has become a culturally diverse city. On a typical Sunday morning, approximately 650 people worship at Cliff Temple Baptist Church in north Oak Cliff, a suburb of Dallas. At the same time, about 850 of their members—many who are recent immigrants—are praying, preaching, and singing in their native languages according to their various cultures in twenty-six small satellite congregations in the church's neighborhood. This same scenario is also repeated in many other cities sprinkled all across North America.

Why do they meet separately? Will the mother church not allow them to meet with it? The church's pastor, Dr. Dean Dickens, explains: "We've determined that it's better for us to try to meet people's needs where they are rather than trying to get them to come into a church which is too big, too white, too affluent and too imposing. The church doesn't have any problem if they want to worship with us, but many of them are more comfortable when we meet them on their turf rather than asking them to show up on our turf."[2] The strategy is to minister to newcomers in their own languages and cultural contexts rather than trying to integrate them into white, Anglo, middle-class congregations.

In the same article, the Rev. Tim Ahlen, consultant for multihousing missions for the Dallas Baptist Association, observes: "And it's very difficult, in terms of congregationalizing folks, because of their different traditions and backgrounds and cultural expressions, to get them in churches together for any extended period. It's kind of funny. They all try to do the right thing and get along together, but they usually wind up going pretty much along national or cultural lines."[3]

If you desire to target people who are different ethnically and culturally from you or your congregation and want them to meet and worship in the same service with you, then you will need to make some changes. So often churches desire to reach people who are different but on their own terms. For example, on one occasion a fellow professor's wife mentioned to me that she wished that her church (a white, Anglo, middle-class, suburban Bible church) would minister to African Americans and Hispanics in the same congregation. I responded by asking her, "What are you willing to give up?" She said, "Beg your pardon?" I asked, "Would you be willing to allow your pastor to hoop (I explained to her that this is an African-American preaching style.) rather than lecturing or using a typical unemotional expository preaching style?" She said, "No." I asked, "Would you be willing to be involved in an offering walk rather than simply passing the plate?" I explained to her this was the way some African-American congregations collect the offering. The collection plate is located on a table at the front of the church. The people walk up to the front and place their money in the plate under the watchful eye of the pastor. Her response of silence told me that she was not ready to go that far to target and reach people who are different.

My experience with affinity has been threefold. First, initially your church will attract people who are most like those in the church—those in the cultural majority. Over time, it will attract others. However, if it attracts people who are different ethnically or culturally, then most likely they are giving up much of their cultural heritage for something that you have to offer them such as good Bible teaching. Second, the pastor will attract those who are most like him. This is especially true of age—a younger pastor will attract young people. An older pastor will attract older people. This is also true of culture and ethnicity. That is why missionaries seek to turn over their works as soon as possible to national pastors. Third, your church will attract those who like your particular style of worship, teaching, and preaching, which may reflect cultural preference.

The examples of organizations and churches that have followed a target group approach are numerous. Christian Associates International, a church planting mission located in Thousand Oaks, California, has targeted Western Europe for church planting. In particular, they are targeting English-speaking internationals located all over Europe. Consequently, their churches consist of racially and culturally diverse people who all understand and speak at least one common language—English. In the same category is the ministry of a Chinese pastor, Arnold Wong, who planted the Asian American Baptist Church in Richardson, Texas. This church targets not Chinese or Korean people, but all Asians who speak English and live in and around Richardson.

A different example is Tim Ahlen and the Country Church that meets in a steakhouse in Mesquite, Texas. This ministry targets those who like country and western music. In its mission statement, the church says that it is "in love with Christian country and Southern gospel music" and "committed to the Lordship of Christ." The music pastor stated, "We wanted to start a New Testament church that would have an appreciation for country, Christian country, and gospel music. I just felt like some of the traditional churches weren't making music as relevant and exciting as it could be. Music is a real common bond."[4]

Most church and parachurch ministries target a specific group of people whether they are aware of it or not. When a church determines its particular cultural style of worship and music as well as other areas, it will attract those who identify with and prefer that cultural style. Most if not all Christian education programs in the church target people when they provide separate classes for singles, couples, children, adults, youth, young marrieds, and newcomers. Why does not the church mix the youth classes with the older adult classes? The answer is that they do not share the same interests. Also, Child Evangelism Fellowship targets children, and Campus Crusade for Christ targets college students, while International Students targets international students who are studying at various schools and colleges in America.

Will You Target Needy People?

The key to unlocking closed minds and touching callused hearts is the convicting ministry of the Holy Spirit (John 16:8–11). However, one way the Spirit convicts people is through addressing their felt needs, as the Savior demonstrated countless times by such acts as physical healing (Matt. 15:30–31) and the provision of the loaves and fishes (John 6). Addressing and providing for one another's needs, especially financial needs (Acts 2:45; 2 Cor. 8:14; 9:12), was extremely important in the early church. Paul in Ephesians 4:29 encourages Christians to build up others according to their needs.[5]

When we address lost people's felt needs through the Scriptures, we get their attention just as the Savior did. We discover their felt needs through personal interviews, local newspapers, demographics, and psychographics. Some typical felt needs are help with addictions, marital strife, problems with kids, loneliness, a lack of community, a need for spiritual truth, self-discovery, child rearing, work-related problems, health problems, and many others. Scripture has much to say regarding these problems, and it is important that the church begin to address them.

The key, however, is to move people from their perceived felt needs to their real needs (their spiritual needs). Jesus demonstrates this with the Samaritan woman at the well who had a felt need for water but whose real need was for living water (John 4:10–15). In John 5, he healed an invalid but said little about spiritual truth. However, later the man returned and Jesus warned him to stop sinning or something worse would happen to him (John 5:14–15).

LOCATE THE TARGET GROUP

The first step is to identify the target group. Once they are identified, the next step is to locate them in the ministry community. There are five questions that help to determine the location of your target group. Each functions like a funnel. These questions force you to think big initially but also cause you to become more focused in your efforts toward the end. This approach is for those ministering internationally as well as in North America.

Where in the World?

The first question begins broadly. It asks: Where in the world is your target group? It invites you to think big—to think world. The focus is where it should be—on the world. It asks you to think in terms of countries. This is necessary for those who are considering foreign missions and for those who are not. Since many who will read this book are already ministering in North America, the answer to this first question will be America.

When Faith Chapel Church begins to focus on its target group the answer will take little thought. It will be America. However, by starting big, this approach should cause Faith Chapel to think beyond its own property line to other countries of the world. As they go through this process, they need to ask if they should be targeting not only people in their own ministry area, but people in other countries. In short, they need to think missions. It is proper for them to consider their ministry community first, for the geographical strategy in Acts began in Jerusalem, then to all of Judea and Samaria, and finally to the ends of the earth (Acts 1:8). In time, however, they will need to think and strategize as to how they can have an impact on the rest of the world.

Where in the Country?

The next question narrows the focus somewhat. Once you have selected a country, this question asks you to select some major area within the country. In a smaller country, the focus may be on the direction of the compass such as the northeast or southwest part of the country. In larger countries like those in North America the focus would be on what state in the U.S.A. or what province in Canada.

Faith Chapel Church will need to ask this question. But the answer for them is already predetermined. It is the state of Texas. Those who desire to plant churches will need to ask this question both of North America and other countries.

Where in the State or Province?

This question narrows the choice even further but is for the larger countries. Using America as an example, the answer would be a specific county. Since Faith Chapel Church is located in Dallas County the answer would appear to be Dallas County.

Where in the County?

The initial answer to the question: Where in the county (or province)? would seem to be a city or town. However, in North America other surrounding areas such as the inner city, urban, suburban, and rural areas play an important role in answering this question. An appropriate answer would consider these important places of ministry.

A tool that will help to answer this question is *American Demographics Magazine*. It includes not only demographic information about most states in America but important, insightful information on cities and communities within and around those cities.

Where in the Community?

I use the term *community* here to mean some geographical location within an urban, suburban, or rural area. I view these areas as made up of various communities, and the ministry will need to determine which community is best for them. This is a key question for church planters because they need to consider targeting new, growing communities. The reason is that these communities will need churches, and people who move into these areas are more open to spiritual truth than those living in older, established communities.

The answer to this question for Faith Chapel Church would seem to be obvious: Their present community. At one time the church's community was a suburb. Over time that has changed, and the church is now in an urban community that has become a part of the inner city of Garland, Texas. However, somewhere in the strategy process, the church and its leadership will need to ask what for them will be a difficult question: Is it time to relocate our church to another community?

This question is as emotionally painful as it is difficult. People become attached to facilities such as church buildings. Older members have numerous memories that involve the current facility: their conversion, baptism, wedding or the wedding of a child, activities and events when the church was experiencing better days, and others. People also have given money to a building fund or have been involved in building some part of the facility. In short, this is an emotionally charged issue for most churches. The problem is that people will allow their memories and the feelings those memories stir to overrule their responsibility to minister to and reach the community for Christ.

The answer to the question of locating the target group in the community is: within reasonable driving distance from the ministry's present facility. Win Arn did a study in 1987 on driving time to the church facility. He discovered that 20 percent of the people took from zero to five minutes to drive to the church. Forty percent spent five to fifteen minutes, 23 percent spent fifteen to twenty-five minutes, 6 percent took twenty-five to thirty-five minutes, 5 percent took thirty-five to forty-five minutes, and 3 percent took forty-five minutes plus (fig. 6.1).[6]

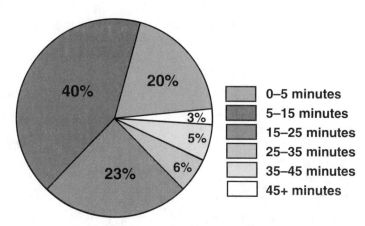

Figure 6.1 Driving Time to Church

A helpful exercise is to draw somewhat concentric circles around your church facility and apply the information from the Arn study. While the figures may vary a little, this exercise will help you to discover the bounds or outer limits of your target community. In an urban area with a substantial expressway or subway system (as in Europe), a person can drive or travel a long distance in fifteen to thirty-five minutes. Also remember, with the invention of the expressway, the parish system is all but dead. In an urban or suburban area, as many people from outside the community could attend your church as live in the community.

Besides these five questions, there are various characteristics of ministry areas that you should also consider in locating the target group. Read through the following and determine which affect your potential target area.

One characteristic mentioned earlier is that older areas are harder to reach than new areas. When people first move into a community, they make one or two critical decisions that affect them spiritually. The first decision is whether they will identify with a church. If the answer is no, then there is no second question. If the answer is yes, the second question is: Which church? Consequently, people in older communities have either decided not to go to church or have already found a church. Another factor is that people in older areas become more set in their ways the longer they live there. They become more change-resistant and thus resist the efforts of those who attempt to reach them for Christ. This does not mean that we ignore these older communities. However, we approach them with different methods and with different expectations than the newer communities.

Another characteristic involves urban areas. People in urban and even inner-city areas range from traditional to nontraditional in their thinking. On the one hand, some are very set in their ways and resist change. This would include those in the older communities just mentioned. On the other hand, others are very open to change. Often this group includes those younger in age and new to the urban community.

A third characteristic affects those in suburban areas. As a general rule, people in suburbia are less traditional. Often the suburban areas tend to be on the fringe of new development. New people are moving into these areas as they are developed. Consequently, they are more open to change and willing to take some risks such as attending a new church in the community.

A fourth characteristic concerns the rural community. With the exception of suburban people who move out to rural areas and commute to and work in the cities, most rural people are more traditional. This means that they are less open to change. However, there are fewer people living in rural America. The flow of the population is from the rural areas to the urban centers of America because that is where people find the better jobs that pay the higher salaries.

One additional suggestion for locating a target group is to conduct a feasibility study. It includes collecting and evaluating such information as a community profile, the existing churches in the community, possible meeting sites, a lifestyle and values survey, as well as other key information.[7]

GATHER INFORMATION ON THE TARGET GROUP

Once you have identified and then located the target group, the third step is to get to know them. To do this, you must gather information on them. The primary tool to accomplish this step is the external audit. At a time when so many churches like Faith Chapel Church are focused inward on themselves and their problems, an external audit forces you to look outward at what is going on in the world and community all around you. Far too many churches go about their business as if their community does not even exist—they are oblivious to it. Auditing the ministry community is not a once-for-all event but must become a regular process if you are to stay in contact with your target group and remain relevant to them. The initial audit takes the most time. It gets easier after that.

What Kind of Information?

Since pastors and churches are in the people business, they need to know well the people in their ministry community. Those businesses that operate in the marketplace are also in the people business, and they know their customers well. A survey of seven thousand people in six countries (Australia, Germany, India, Japan, Great Britain, and the United States) conducted by Sponsorship International of London, England, has revealed that the McDonald's logo—an arched M—and the shell used by the Shell Oil Petroleum Company ranked higher in recognizability than the Christian cross. The survey also found that the five linked rings of the Olympic movement was the most recognized symbol in the survey. Christopher Mayfield, the Anglican Bishop of Manchester, told the *Daily Mail* newspaper in London, "The Olympic movement, Shell and McDonald's have a worldwide vision, so they are to be congratulated on getting their message across to the world. Christianity also has a worldwide vision, but we have not been so successful in communicating the faith, and we have got to do better."[8] How have McDonald's and Shell Oil achieved such marketability? They have a vision and a strategy to accomplish that vision that involves knowing their customer. Pastor Rick Warren spent three years studying the Mission Viejo, California, community before planting Saddleback Community Church, which now numbers more than ten thousand people. There are at least four primary sources of profile information: demographics, psychographics, trends, and history.

Demographics

Demographics provides certain basic information about the people who make up the target group such as age, sex, education, occupation, income, race, marital status, and other areas. This knowledge helps the church to discover its potential "customers" and what they are like. The following are some demographic segments that will help you and your ministry to discover, categorize, and understand your target group:

1. Age: Pre-Boomers or Builders (before 1946), Boomers (1946–64), or Busters (also called Generation Xers; 1965–83)
2. Sex: male, female
3. Race or ethnicity: White, Black, Hispanic, Asian, and others
4. Language: English, Spanish, Chinese, Korean, and others
5. Types of households: single-parent, dual-parent, and so on
6. Education: none, elementary, high school, college, graduate school
7. Income: lower, middle, upper
8. Housing: apartment dweller, home owner
9. Occupation: collar color (blue- and white-collar occupations)

10. Marital status: single, married, separated, or divorced
11. Religion: Protestant, Catholic, Jewish, Muslim, and others

Where do you get demographic information? There are two sources: primary and secondary. Primary sources are local sources. They are the most accurate. You may obtain them from public libraries, utilities, realtors, real estate organizations, chambers of commerce, city and county planning offices, zoning boards, universities, colleges, newspapers, commercial developers, door-to-door surveys, as well as personal observation.

Secondary sources are national sources. They have general reliability. However, many rely on the census that is taken every decade. Consequently, the information becomes less reliable toward the middle and end of each decade. You would be wise to confirm them with some local information. National sources include various professional organizations that provide their services for a price. Some of these are CACI Source Products of Fairfax, Virginia; National Decisions Systems of Encinitas, California; Panoramic Area Ministry of Pasadena, California. A Christian organization mentioned earlier that specializes in demographics for ministries is Church Information and Development Services (CIDS) of Costa Mesa, California.

Psychographics

Psychographics presents information about what people are looking for in life. It is all about people's needs, values, desires, beliefs, hopes, dreams, aspirations, fears, and so on. Psychographic studies ask: What is important to them? What are their concerns? and How are these things changing?

Psychographic information helps you to answer certain questions such as: Do you know and understand the needs of those in your target group? Are you addressing people's needs, values, and hopes? How well? Can you meet these needs? Should you even attempt to satisfy their needs? Which needs? While you cannot meet all the needs, you can meet some. Identify the ones you can meet. What would a satisfied "customer" look like? What will it take for your ministry to address some of the needs, values, and dreams?

Where will you get psychographic information? Several sources exist.

One is to ask people for the information. This could take the form of a survey. It is important that you make a point of listening to your customers (target group). Practice naive listening. Knocking on doors is difficult, but you can find these people in shopping malls where they are more accessible and willing to answer your questions than from behind a closed door in their neighborhood. Also, contact area businesses—they may have already done much of the work for you. And because you are a ministry, they may provide the information for free.

Another source of psychographic information is observation. Observe people; watch what they do. You can learn a lot by simply studying the habits of the people you are trying to reach. Do you see them at the local parks? What are they doing there? What other places do they frequent and why? Spend some of your time observing people at the local mall.

Other sources are local periodicals, newspapers, and professional organizations such as those mentioned under demographics that may also provide psychographic information for a fee.

Trends

You must ask: What are the dominant trends affecting the target group? You should probe the following areas for the trends that affect each:

1. Social: crime, racial issues, abortion, pornography, abuse, local schools, and others
2. Technological: computer, fax, cellular phones, and so on
3. Economic: jobs, recession, inflation, layoffs, opportunities, prime rate, and others
4. Political: national, state, and local issues
5. Religious: the growing number of unchurched, the influence of Promise Keepers on men, the advance of Islam. What do people believe about the Bible, angels, prayer, and other biblical issues? Gallup and Barna surveys can be helpful. How do these surveys apply to your target area?

Try to determine how your target group is responding to these trends if at all. How might your church or ministry address these issues? What difference could you make?

Where will you find information on trends? One good source is books such as John Naisbitt's *Megatrends* and *Megatrends 2000*. Other sources are television, newspapers, and periodicals.

History

Is there anything taking place historically that might affect your target group? At the end of the twentieth century, as we move into the twenty-first century, we are at a hinge in history. The modern era is passing and the postmodern era has arrived. The Enlightenment strongly influenced the modern era in America and was the major contributor to rampant secularism. The question is whether the postmodern era will bring more of the same, or will there be a revival of traditional values? This has not proved to be the case in Western Europe.

An awareness of historical events may directly or indirectly affect the success or survival of your ministry, especially at the local level. They may positively or negatively have an impact on your ability to achieve your ministry mission. The other option is to assume the position of the proverbial ostrich with its head in the sand. The problem is that this posture leaves you totally exposed. The failure to keep current has buried numerous churches and businesses.

CONSTRUCT A PROFILE PERSON

The last step in determining your target group is to construct a profile person. This involves collecting and then synthesizing all the target group information you gathered in steps one, two, and three into one composite description. From this information, you construct a profile person that summarizes all the characteristics of your target person.

The primary purpose for creating the profile person is twofold. First, it helps communicate to all in the ministry as well as staff and board who it is that you are trying to reach. They may or may not be people who are much like those who make up the ministry. For example, Faith Chapel Church may want to target a younger group of people. If they desire to reach those in their immediate community, then they will need to target a different ethnic group. In their case this might be a Hispanic person.

Second, the profile person also serves as a constant reminder that you have a target—a group of people that you are trying to reach for Christ. It takes about a month for a congregation to forget the ministry's vision. I believe that it also takes approximately the same time to forget whom you are trying to reach because the mission and the target group are so closely related. The quality development process of a profile person will keep your target person before the church.

You will also need to determine what the profile person will look like. This person could be a man or a woman or both. You could give the person or persons a name. Saddleback Community Church has created "Saddleback Sam." Willow Creek Community Church has created "Unchurched Harry and Mary." I developed "Duncanville Dan" as a profile person for Duncanville, Texas, a suburb of Dallas, Texas. He is a slice of white-collar, middle-class America. "Oak Cliff Cliff," however, is a profile of the typical person in Oak Cliff, Texas, another suburb of Dallas. A plumber, he depicts blue-collar people who make up the working class of America.

The profile person could be a cartoon character like "Duncanville Dan" or "Oak Cliff Cliff," or a normal character. You might dress this person in clothing that is characteristic of your community. I dressed "Duncanville Dan" in a suit and tie because that is what he wears in corporate America, while I dressed "Oak Cliff Cliff" in the typical plumber's garb. If the people are highly interested in golf or tennis, put a golf club or a tennis racquet in one hand.

QUESTIONS FOR DISCUSSION AND REFLECTION

1. Is your ministry attempting to reach everyone in general (the shotgun method) or a smaller segment of people (the rifle method)? Is it working? Why or why not?

2. Does your ministry realize that it is in the people business? What is your church's general attitude toward people—good or bad? What is your attitude toward people? Do visitors find the ministry warm and friendly, and do they come back? What does this say about the possibility of reaching people?

3. Is your church targeting saved or lost people or both? Why or why not? Are you targeting churched or unchurched people? If the former, what is your reputation in the community—good or bad? Why? Is your ministry targeting seekers? Why or why not? What is your church's approach to seekers? In which category would you place your church: seeker-driven, seeker-friendly, seeker-tolerant, or seeker-hostile? Why?

4. Is your ministry willing to reach anybody and everybody? Why or why not? If the answer is no, who is not welcome? Is it reaching anybody and everybody? If not, whom is it reaching? Why? Who realistically can you reach, who will most likely respond to your ministry? Why?

5. Is your church meeting people at a need's level? Which people— lost or saved? What needs? What needs should you be addressing but are not? What needs can you legitimately address?

6. Where is your target group located? Is it within reasonable driving distance of your ministry facility? How long would it take for someone in the target area to drive to your facility? Is the target community an older or younger area? What difference will the age of the area make? Is it located in an urban, suburban, or rural area? What difference will this make?

7. Answer the following questions if you have gathered demographic information on your target community. What age is your target group? What sex? What race? What language do they speak? More than one language? What type of household? How much education? Income level? Type of housing? What kind of occupations? What is their marital status? What is their religious status?

8. What do the people in your target group value? What are their hopes, dreams, and aspirations? How do you know? Do you listen to people in your target area? Have you spent any time observing them? Why or why not?

9. What are some of the dominant trends affecting your target group? How do you know? How might these affect your ministry? What, if anything, can you do about them?

10. What of historical significance is taking place internationally that would in some way affect your target group or your ministry to them? Nationally? Locally? How might this affect your ministry?

11. Do you believe that constructing a profile person would help your people to understand and reach your target community? Why or why not? What name might you select for your target person or persons?

ENDNOTES

1. See the sections in chapter 4, pp. 58–63, on form, function, and freedom.

2. Bryan Woolley, "Ministering to Immigrants," *The Dallas Morning News*, November 4, 1995, p. 1A.

3. Ibid., p. 30A.

4. "Place of Worship," *The Dallas Morning News*, August 12, 1995, p. 2G.

5. Some Christians speak out against addressing people at the need level. They refer to it as a humanistic, man-centered approach to evangelism and missions. This attitude sounds very spiritual; however, I find this mind-set frightening as well as unbiblical.

6. Win Arn, "Driving Time to Church," *The Win Arn Growth Report*, Pasadena, Calif., vol. 1, no. 20.

7. See Aubrey Malphurs, *Planting Growing Churches for the 21st Century* (Grand Rapids, Mich.: Baker Book House, 1992), pp. 361–67, for a sample that is used in church planting.

8. "Study: McDonald's Logo More Recognizable Than Christian Cross," *The Dallas/Fort Worth Heritage*, October 1995, p. 6.

CHAPTER SEVEN

The Program of the Strategy

ASKING THE CRUCIAL QUESTIONS

*". . . men of Issachar, who understood the times and knew what
Israel should do."*   —1 Chronicles 12:32

If you had asked the typical member of Faith Chapel Church in the
1940s or 1950s whom they were attempting to reach for Christ, he or
she would have paused, looked puzzled for a moment, then smiled and
said: "Why everyone, of course."

Had you examined the membership, however, you would have
observed mostly young, white, middle-class families. They were Ozzie-
and-Harriet types whom you could count on to be there every Sunday.
Families dressed in their Sunday best and sat proudly together, enduring
the same unpadded wood pew week after week. Over the years, they
have enjoyed growing old together. Their only disappointment is that
their kids have not proved to be as faithful to the Chapel as they have.
Most of their children now live in the suburbs and no longer make the
long drive back to the church. If they attend church at all, then they have
opted to attend one of the megachurches in their own communities that
offers a broader ministry menu with numerous programs for them and
their kids.

Pastor Robert Smith worked long and hard in an attempt to identify a
target group for Faith Chapel Church. There were several options. One
was to target the numerous low-income Hispanic families who now
populate the immediate community surrounding the church. However,
Pastor Robert knew that Faith Chapel would have to become a Hispanic
church culturally to accomplish this, and the congregation would not
survive such a drastic change. Another option was to sell the church
facility to the growing Hispanic church that was meeting in Faith Chapel's

111

facility Sunday afternoons. Then Faith Chapel would relocate to one of the newer, growing suburbs of Garland where it might target younger families.

No one liked either option but there seemed to be no other viable one. After much discussion, the board decided that the second option, though painful, was in the best interests of the church. Consequently, they brought their decision to the congregation for discussion and, in time, a vote. They wisely held numerous open discussion meetings, and let everyone have a say. The congregation was not happy with the board's choice, and some felt betrayed, but most agreed that it was their only choice outside of maintaining the status quo until the eventual death of the church. A few stalwarts sincerely believed that death was preferable and less painful than selling their building and moving to another location. They had contributed substantially to building the church facility, and it held many wonderful memories for them. Regardless, when the vote finally came, it was unanimous that the Chapel should move.

However, other important decisions and significant changes lie ahead for Faith Chapel. The initial decision was to move and target a younger generation of people. That would be much harder than anyone, including Pastor Robert, had ever imagined. The question they had to answer now was: What kind of church will it take to reach the new target group when we move to the new community? Their search for an answer proved for many to be both the best of times and the worst of times.

———————

Chapter 6 has taken you through the second step, the process of identifying your target group. It has helped you to answer the question: Who are we going to reach for Christ? I have designed this chapter to help you and your ministry take the third step. Like Faith Chapel, you must answer the question: What kind of church will it take to reach your target group? This is a critical strategy question as you will discover in the next chapter. This chapter also heavily immerses you in the process of strategy development as you work toward the product—your initial strategy. It involves a theology of change and rests heavily on the material on form, function, and freedom in chapter 4. Answer the following questions for your church. Your answers to these questions will dictate much of your strategy and provide the nuts and bolts that will make up your strategy.

Answering the question concerning the kind of church necessary to reach your target group calls for much creativity. To jumpstart your creativity, there are two other questions that you may begin with before you consider your target group. The first is: What kind of ministries are reaching people around the world and in America? The second is: What kind of ministries are reaching people in your community?

WHAT KIND OF MINISTRIES ARE REACHING PEOPLE AROUND THE WORLD AND IN AMERICA?

I have purposely used the term *ministries* because I include parachurch ministries in the following discussion. As difficult as it is for some pastors and church leaders to admit, a number of these groups have come into existence to meet the shortcomings of local churches. While none of these parachurch organizations are perfect, we can learn much from them. Consequently, each section will explore not only the world's of the exemplary and struggling churches, but will include the parachurch ministries as well.

The Exemplary Church Ministries

Another way of asking this first question is: What are the disciple-making churches outside your ministry area doing? To answer this question, you should be aware of what is taking place on the international and national church scene. Become a student of the exemplary churches around the world and in North America.

There are many exemplary churches that can give you general insight into and ideas for your ministry strategy. Here are just a few examples: Yoido Full Gospel Church, the world's largest church, located in Korea; Willow Creek Community Church, Barrington, Illinois; Saddleback Community Church, Mission Viejo, California; Grace Community Church, Sun Valley, California; Bear Valley Church, Denver, Colorado; Wooddale Church, Eden Prairie, Minnesota; Grace Community Church, Baltimore, Maryland; Perimeter Church, Atlanta, Georgia; Spring Creek Community Church, Garland, Texas; and Oak Cliff Bible Fellowship, Dallas, Texas.

How do you find out about these churches? Some of the pastors have written books on their ministries. A local Christian bookstore will help you to locate them. John Vaughn has written books on the world's largest and fastest-growing churches, and you may subscribe to his publication entitled *Church Growth Today*.[1] Another source is word of mouth. Talk to other pastors in your area, to associations, or to other denominations and explore with them some of the examples that they might be familiar with.

As you discover these ministries and learn more about them, you should look for what your ministry might have in common with them. How can they help you? What can you learn about ministry from them? For example, do you have a similar style of ministry, target group, community, vision, mission, core values, problems, existing congregations, and so on? In particular, discover the forms they are using to implement their functions (evangelism, worship, communication, and others). Large ministries can learn much from Yoido Full Gospel Church. How do you minister to and shepherd all those people in a large church? Yoido Full Gospel Church is a church of small or cell groups, each of which has its own pastor. Some argue that this church, the world's largest, ministers better to their people than most small churches.

Another area that could be most helpful to your church is technology. Ask the question: What technology are they using to accomplish their ministry? Are they using computers, slide-tape presentations, video productions, audio tape ministries, laser printers, fax machines, cellular phones, and so on? How could these enhance your ministry?

The Parachurch Ministries

Next, you should explore what the parachurch ministries are doing. This, too, will involve discovering the parachurch ministries that serve in North America and around the world. Some of the more well-known ones are the Navigators, Campus Crusade, Promise Keepers, the Gideons, Touch Ministries, Serendipity, Stephen's Ministries, Focus on the Family, and many others.

Traditionally, parachurch organizations have sprung up to target people that the churches have not reached and to accomplish ministries that churches have neglected. Two examples are evangelism and discipleship. Consequently, the church can learn much from the parachurch movement about reaching people and what the church should and could be doing as well as how to do it.

Since the mission of the church is to make disciples, you should study carefully those parachurch ministries that focus on disciple making and are good at it such as the Navigators, Equipping the Saints, and Campus Crusade for Christ. Ask: What can they teach us about making disciples? Learn how they evangelize and worship and how they are developing leaders. Ask: Who are their unique target groups? How are they similar to us? What are they doing that could help us? How could we help them?

The Struggling Church Ministries

According to Win Arn, 80 to 85 percent of the churches in America (and I would suspect North America) are plateaued or in decline. Schaller writes that two-thirds to three-fourths of all congregations founded before 1960 are either on a plateau or shrinking in numbers.[2] Perhaps not all but many of these churches are struggling ministries. Many are like Faith Chapel Church—they have been around for a long time, are resistant to change, and are still ministering in the past. As many as one-third will not survive the 1990s, and a significant number of those who do will expire early in the twenty-first century.

In these difficult or declining situations, one can learn something; unfortunately, one usually learns a lot about what not to do and what God is not blessing. I came to faith in Christ around age nineteen and have been excited about it ever since. God also gave me a love and passion for the local church, but my early experiences were primarily in churches that were dysfunctional and struggling. Somehow I realized that something was wrong and decided to learn whatever I could about serving the Savior in these difficult situations. Most of my models were seriously flawed, and I learned a lot about how not to lead and relate to people.

Learning what not to do is helpful but insufficient for ministry in the twenty-first century. It is more important that we learn what to do than what not to do. We learn what to do from good models—the churches that God is blessing—not from the ineffective ones. This is why it is so important for seminarians and those preparing for ministry to invest a significant amount of their time in church-related ministries, but not in just any ministry. Wise future leaders in their formative preparations for ministry will look for churches that are functional and modeling Christlike ministry, not those that are dysfunctional, discouraged, and out of touch. That does not mean that they will not opt to minister in a dysfunctional church in the future, but it is best not to do so in the formative times of early ministry leadership and development when one needs a positive ministry model.

WHAT KIND OF MINISTRIES ARE REACHING PEOPLE IN YOUR MINISTRY AREA?

Studying and staying current on the ministries around the world and particularly in North America will be most enlightening. They will serve to put muscle on your creative abilities and give you ideas that could have a profound impact on your ministry. However, you must also explore ministries close to home because they signal what may or may not work in your unique ministry environment.

The Exemplary Church Ministries

The next step is to ask: Who are the disciple-making churches in your area? What are they doing that God is blessing? You would serve your church well by getting to know these ministries and their people. They have a proven track record, and they have probably made some bad decisions as well as some good ones along the way. It is wise to learn from them so that you do not repeat their mistakes while benefiting from their wise choices.

I live in the Dallas-Fort Worth metroplex area. As I survey this ministry landscape, I see a number of churches that God is blessing. The following are only a few: Spring Creek Community Church, Oak Cliff Bible Fellowship, Pantego Bible Church, Reinhardt Bible Church, Prestonwood Baptist Church, Fellowship Bible Church of Dallas, Lakepointe Baptist Church, Irving Bible Church, Los Colinas Fellowship, Concord Missionary Baptist Church, Asian American Baptist Church, Christ Church North, West Lake Community Church, Lakewood Assembly of God, St. Luke Community Church, Antioch Fellowship Baptist Church, as well as others. While I might not agree with the theology of each and every one these churches, I have discovered that I can learn much about ministry from them and their leaders. When eating fish—one eats the meat and tosses away the skin and bones. As you survey your ministry landscape, what churches can you learn from, deriving the best "meat" from their experiences?

How do you find out about these churches? Some of the pastors have written books, and some of the churches sponsor a pastors' conference. However, the best approach is to network with these pastors. Make an appointment with them or take them to lunch. If they are too busy, then pursue a staff associate. Some of them also attend pastoral gatherings or belong to pastors' associations in their areas—join them.

As you discover what they are doing, ask what their ministries have in common with yours. Do you serve the same kind of people in terms of education, collar color, income, and so on? Do you share a similar philosophy of ministry? It would be a major mistake, or course, if you attempt to mimic or replicate their church in every way. The goal is to find transferable lessons from their experience that apply to your unique situation.

The Parachurch Ministries

You should also explore what the parachurch ministries are doing in your area. Many of those with whom you are not already familiar can be found in the phone book. Focus on those who are serving in ministry areas that are typical of your church, such as evangelism, discipleship, and so on. If they are willing to help you, you can also be of help to them.

Again, the key to this is networking. Carve a certain amount of time out of your schedule every week for networking. Get to know as many leaders as possible. Christ's disciples practiced networking: "One of the men was Andrew. . . . The first thing Andrew did was to find his brother, Simon. . . . The next day Jesus . . . found Philip. . . . Philip found Nathaniel and told him" (John 1:40–44).

The Struggling Church Ministries

Next ask: What are the struggling churches in your area doing or not doing? What is God not blessing? Meet with these pastors as time permits. Take advantage of any chance meetings (you find yourself standing behind one at the drugstore or meet a fellow pastor at a school function). Ask them as many questions as possible—with tact and consideration, of course! Offer encouragement to those who are struggling.

What can you learn from them? Why are they struggling? What are some of the mistakes they or their churches have made that will help you not to repeat the same? Where can you find these churches? In the churched South there is one on every block and several in every neighborhood. The Midwest will have long-standing church ministries in towns, villages, and rural areas. You will find fewer of them in the unchurched Northeast and Northwest, but they are there.

WHAT KIND OF CHURCH WILL IT TAKE TO REACH YOUR TARGET GROUP?

In this last section, you will answer a number of questions designed to help you think through and determine what timely, relevant forms or methods your church should adopt to target its community while ministering to its people. Here is where you will also pull together the insights and ideas you gained from the international, national, and other local ministries and creatively apply them to your ministry.

The result of following this process will be your product or initial strategy. I use the term *initial* because it will not be your final strategy. You will not produce a final strategy because you will always be adjusting it. Your strategy is like a sophisticated race car engine. It will need constant adjustment and fine tuning if it is to hit on all its cylinders.

It is a major mistake to attempt to implement the entire strategy immediately unless you are planting a church. The typical established church such as Faith Chapel would not survive such a drastic change. However, the value of having a completed strategy is that you know where you are going and how you will eventually arrive there. Then it becomes a matter not of *what* you should do (you have already decided this) but *when* you should do it. It is a matter of timing the implementation of the strategy.

You should also consider how pre-Boomers or Builders (those born before 1946), Boomers (1946–64), and Busters or Generation X (1965–83) in America respond to these forms.[3] They will make up your present ministry and target group. A recognition of these three generations and the distinctive tastes and expectations of each is important to implementing your strategy. Consequently, I have included some generational applications below. These applications will characterize approximately three-fourths of those who make up each generation.[4]

Some have labeled the next generation that is now forming (1984 to present) the Echo Boom. Not much information is available on them at this time. You would be wise to remain alert to them as well because they may be present in your current ministry and are its future. Ask yourself: Will you lose or keep them? What will it take to reach them?

The pastor or point person in the church should first work through the following questions on his own so that he knows his preferences. Then either he, a consultant, or a wise, skillful board member should lead the pastoral staff, board, and other important leaders through the same questions. Where there are strong differences, strive for a consensus, not a compromise.

What Kind of Meetings?

The church by definition involves a gathering of people. Thus, the church meets together in various ways, at various times, and in various sized groups. Concerning size, it has three options: the large group meeting, medium-sized group meeting, and the small group meeting.

The Large Group Meeting

Most churches have at least one meeting where everyone gathers. Pastors and leaders must ask and answer a number of questions about this meeting. What are you trying to accomplish with this meeting? What is its purpose: teaching, preaching, discipleship, evangelism, inspiration, celebration, worship, or a combination thereof? Can you accomplish more than one purpose with this meeting?

Is your purpose for the meeting feasible? For example, most teaching churches attempt to disciple people at the large group meeting through a sermon. The question is: Can you depend on preaching to a large group or on a teaching session to make disciples? In today's culture (even in the Bible Belt), most people attend church on average two to three times a month, and some people attend more than one church.

All three generational groups like to attend a large group meeting. Some, like seekers, prefer the anonymity it provides. It allows them to come and seek God, hear the Word of God, or just check things out.

The Medium-Sized Group Meeting

Peter Wagner believes that the ideal size for this meeting is 30 to 80 people. It can grow to 100 or 120 but at this size it begins to lose a sense of fellowship.[5] You should ask several question of this format. What is the purpose for this meeting? Larger churches have used the medium-sized group for Sunday school classes, especially those that employ the lecture format. Some have used them to form mini-congregations within the larger congregation. Others have creatively used them as an opportunity to pull together all their small groups for a time of teaching under a master teacher or for a seminar on evangelism, Bible study methods, parenting, and other topics.

All three generational groups may enjoy the medium-sized group. It all depends on what you do with them. Builders tend to prefer this size because it lends itself to the lecture format. They prefer more content and less interaction on a personal level. Boomers and Busters prefer this size especially if the speaker is an expert on the topic. But they also want the personal interaction that a small group provides.

The Small Group Meeting

The ideal size of a small group is approximately ten people.[6] A small group is an excellent environment for evangelism, community, teaching, worship, leadership training, prayer, and other functions. It is where you can best accomplish the Bible's "one another" exhortations. It is where transformation or life change best takes place. It is decidedly the best context for making disciples! Some choose to celebrate the ordinances in the small group meetings as well.

There are several kinds of small groups: service or task groups, growth or discipleship groups (children, teens, men and women—all together or separately), and support groups (Alcoholics Anonymous, Al-Anon, Mothers of Preschoolers, bereavement and grief support groups, and others).

Leaders such as Lyman Coleman, Roberta Hestenes, Ralph Neighbour, Carl George, and Dale Galloway have all published a number of works and contributed much to small group or cell-group ministries around the world.

The generational groups respond differently to the small group meeting. The Baby Boomers and Busters prefer small group meetings. They sense a deep need for community. Most desire to interact on a more personal level. The Builders tend to avoid small groups, especially the men. I believe that for many it is a masculinity issue. Builders view real men as strong, silent, and unemotional. You keep your pain and personal problems to yourself. Many small group programs are designed to surface pain and problems, not hide them.

What Kind of Worship?

What kind of worship style will your church adopt? Will you attempt a more traditional style, a contemporary style, or both?

Traditional Worship

The grand old hymns of the faith, hymnals, choirs with robes, the organ and piano, and so on characterize traditional worship. It is slow-paced, quieter, longer, more formal, reverent, and may at times involve the worshipper more in observation than participation. In some situations, the choir may lead and even do much of the worship. In traditional worship services, people learn and sing about God. The Builders prefer this style of worship. They have always worshipped this way.

Contemporary Worship

Praise and worship songs, a band, synthesizer, slides, videos, and either a choir without robes or no choir at all characterize contemporary worship. It is fast-paced, louder than traditional worship, may be shorter or longer, more casual, celebrative, upbeat, and more participative. More than learning and singing about God, people sing to and worship God. For example, you can sing about God's love as expressed in many traditional hymns, or you can tell him that you love him as expressed in many praise songs. The Boomers and Busters prefer a more contemporary style. They feel that they can relate to the contemporary sound much better than to traditional music styles.

As the church closes out the twentieth century and enters the twenty-first century, the choice of a worship style has become a divisive issue. However, traditionalists must realize that today's traditional music was yesterday's contemporary music while contemporists must understand that today's contemporary music will be tomorrow's traditional worship music!

It may be wise not to attempt to blend both styles in the same worship service. When you mix them, both generational groups complain. However, to pick one style over another alienates the group not picked. If you are forced to choose one style over another, you may want to choose the more contemporary style because you must reach the future generations, or the church will die. If the size of the church allows for it, then the best solution is to schedule two services, one traditional and the other contemporary.

A current debate is whether to use so-called secular music in the service. The original purpose of the music and the lyrics are key issues in determining the appropriateness of using such music. My observation is that secular music can sometimes be used with the sermon in an illustrative manner or to make a key point. It is difficult to believe, however, that it can contribute to worship. Someone might take a secular melody, however, and add Christian lyrics just as John and Charles Wesley did with secular tunes in the eighteenth century. Be aware, however, that a copyrighted musical tune cannot be used without written permission. Several churches have learned very painfully that appropriating material without permission, and in some cases payment, can result in costly legal problems.

What Kind of Community?

For many in the typical, traditional church, "community" has consisted of somewhat surface relationships experienced while standing around in the foyer after church, standing in line at the local cafeteria, or sitting in a Sunday school class or at a church potluck or social. It is community at arms' length. This type of community is characteristic of the church in the first half of the twentieth century. It is what many Builders or pre-Boomers prefer, especially the men. Often for these men it is a "masculinity" issue—the typical Builder male was raised to be a rugged individualist who needs no one.

Authentic community, however, consists of relating to one another up close, openly, and in depth. People are accepted as they are, and it is okay not to be "okay." The community does not demand perfection as the price of acceptance. It involves living and experiencing the "one another" passages of the Bible such as love one another, encourage one another, teach one another, and so forth. Much of it takes place during the weekly small group meetings and in the relationships that spin off them. The Boomers and Xers value and prefer this kind of community.

What Kind of Teaching?

Good, expository Bible teaching must be a vital function of every church. Few would debate this. At issue is: Who does the teaching? Some churches prefer that the professional staff and a few lay people do all the teaching. Others involve more lay persons.

The Professional Staff as the Teachers

In the more traditional type churches, professionals do most of the teaching. As one old-timer at Faith Chapel remarked: "After all, that's what we pay them to do!" Many also argue that the professionals are the ones with all the training. The goal of teaching is primarily to inform— if you tell people what to do, they will do it. The Builders have become accustomed to this style.

In some traditional and in a growing number of new paradigm churches, the professionals function in two ways. They teach in the large group and middle-sized groups. They also focus on training and equipping gifted lay persons to do much of the teaching in a small group context. Thus, a small group might have a leader with the gift of teaching, or some gifted leader may lead while a gifted teacher teaches. This training could be in-depth, including the original languages for those interested. Most Boomers and Busters along with some Builders prefer this approach to teaching.

The Laity as the Teachers

In the classical, traditional church, lay persons are often viewed primarily as students who are there to learn the Bible. Teaching is limited to a few gifted lay people in a middle-sized group context. It takes place in the Sunday school classroom at church and often follows a lecture format with some time at the end for questions and interaction. The Builders have become accustomed to this approach.

In the new-paradigm approach, gifted lay persons do actual in-depth teaching in small groups that meet all over the city. The staff has trained them to do much of the teaching. The goal is to transform as well as inform. The Boomers and Xers often prefer this approach.

What Kind of Evangelism?

As is true with teaching, some churches prefer that professionals evangelize. Others encourage more lay involvement while some attempt both.

The Professionals Evangelize

At churches like Faith Chapel, the pastor, itinerant evangelists, and missionaries traditionally do most, if not all, of the evangelism. It takes place primarily in large groups at a church service, a special revival meeting at the church, or going door-to-door in the community. The Builder generation prefers this approach. A key question that these churches ask about their evangelistism programs and events is: How much will they cost?

In many of the newer ministries, pastors, professional evangelists, and missionaries not only evangelize but model and train others to do so. The key question is not: How much does it cost, but, Do lost people matter? (Luke 15; Mark 8:36). The Boomers and Busters are most concerned about their lost friends and neighbors. They want someone to train them so they can share Christ effectively.

The Laity Evangelize

In many older churches, lay persons encourage the professionals in their evangelistic efforts and support them. They may act as "bringers" (they bring the lost to hear their pastor or an evangelist). Some lay people are trained to evangelize, however, using a more confrontational style.

In newer churches, lay people discover their evangelism style and share Christ accordingly. Evangelism often takes place in the context of a small group. The leader of the small group provides an empty chair and encourages people to bring a lost person who will occupy it at the next meeting. Some groups conduct an evangelistic project once a month such as holding a free car wash, mowing and raking someone's yard, or other similar projects. This particular project is only for people outside the church, not those already a part of it. Another approach is to invite lost friends to a large group seeker-service designed with them in mind.

What Kind of Missions?

Promote Foreign Missions

A number of the old paradigm churches have promoted foreign missions almost exclusively. Many of the traditional church members believe that America is a Christian nation; therefore, they feel they must focus the church's missions efforts on foreign missions. The extent of their involvement is writing a check, praying for missionaries, providing hospitality for a visiting missionary family in their home, and attending the yearly missions conferences. This approach largely characterizes the Builder generation.

Promote Home and Local Missions As Well As Foreign Missions

Some traditional churches and many of the new paradigm churches that have been planted in the last twenty years take a more balanced view. They believe that both America and the rest of the world are mission fields. They may not be as involved in foreign missions, and the extent of that involvement is supporting missionaries and taking short-term mission trips abroad. They enjoy involvement in a local mission project or church planting. This characterizes the Boomers and Xers who tend not to give as much money to missions as the Builders.

What Kind of Leadership?

The Role of Professional Leadership

In the larger, old-style churches, the "pros" (staff) do much of the leading—they are the trained, salaried professionals who are highly competent to do the work of the ministry. They also lead because of their position. As one church patriarch put it: "We follow the pastor because he *is* the pastor." This typically characterizes the pre-Boomer generation.

In the newer churches, the staff functions more as coaches to train other gifted leaders and lay people (the top 25 percent) to lead and do the work of the ministry. They are heavily involved in mentoring other gifted leaders whether laity or interns. Usually there is an apprentice shadowing them wherever they go. They lead because of their character, vision, and core values. As one Buster put it: "We follow the pastor because he's real!" This characterizes the Busters and Boomers.

The Role of Lay Leadership

In the larger traditional churches, most lay people are followers. They are responsible to attend the services, provide financial support, and follow the leadership. There is a cadre of lower level leaders that staff some of the programs such as Christian education. In the smaller, older, and often more rural churches, a board of trusted old-timers may lead the church, especially if the pastor is young or just out of seminary. In some of the younger churches, lay people are to lead and minister to people. The church considers them as highly qualified for ministry as the pros and uses their professional abilities in such areas as marketing, quality control, advertising, communication, public relations, and so on.

What Kind of Preaching?

What Kind of Sermons

The older paradigm evangelical churches feature longer sermons, lasting from forty-five to sixty minutes. Some expect their pastors to preach an evangelistic sermon every week followed by an invitation to come forward and receive Christ or rededicate one's life to Christ. Traditionally, the teaching churches probe deeply into the biblical text—the primary emphasis is on what the text means. Sermons are mostly extended expositions of the books of the Bible. Topical sermons are considered taboo.

The newer churches feature shorter sermons, lasting twenty to forty minutes, that are both biblical and highly relevant. The primary concern is not only what the text means but its relevance and application to everyday life. They take seriously the text: "Do what it [the Word] says" (James 1:22). Sermons are a combination of topical, expository, and biographical preaching, and some employ an occasional dramatic or narrative sermon.

What Kind of Preacher

In the traditional church, the senior pastor does most, if not all, of the preaching. An associate or assistant may preach when the senior pastor is away or on vacation. People prefer that the preacher not share too much from his personal life, especially his failures, for they need to look up to him as an example or model of what they should be. This is the opinion of many Builders.

A newer approach is to use a team of gifted preachers (two or more) who share the preaching ministry. The team will consist of the point pastor and one or more associate or assistant pastors, depending on the size of the church. Often the point pastor preaches more or slightly more than an associate. It is important that they share from their lives, especially their failures as well as their successes. This is considered authentic preaching. The Boomers and Xers delight in this approach.

What Version of the Bible?

Traditional churches use older versions and selected newer versions such as the King James Version (KJV), the *New King James Version* (NKJV), and the *New American Standard Bible* (NASB). As one old-timer put it, "If the King James Bible was good enough for Jesus and the disciples, then it's good enough for us!" Most of the churches begun after the 1960s to use newer versions such as the NASB and the *New International Version* (NIV). Eugene Peterson's *The Message* is also popular among the Boomers and Busters, most of whom struggle with translations from other cultures and centuries and want a translation with language that they can understand.

What Kind of Communication?

Communication Within the Church

The typical church communicates through announcements, bulletins, and monthly newsletters. Much of the communication is characterized by "temple talk" (1 Cor. 14:23–25). For example, people use biblical terms such as *reconciliation, propitiation, redemption,* and church terms such as *sanctuary, benediction, vestibule,* and *postlude,* which many unchurched people do not understand. Many newer churches use a wide variety of communication techniques afforded by technological advances. Rather than making announcements during the service, a computer, connected to a video projector, flashes the announcements on a screen prior to the service. Another example is that not only do they use bulletins and newsletters, they also use e-mail, fax machines, and teleconferences. They tend to avoid biblical terms and church terms that the contemporary culture might not understand. The typical person who attended church in the first century understood terms such as redemption and reconciliation. They were used commonly in the market places. That is not true in the twentieth century. Contemporary churches might refer to the bulletin as a program, the sermon as a message or talk, and the sanctuary as the auditorium.

Communication Outside the Church

Typically, churches have used "Visitors Welcome" signs in the front yard to communicate with their community. The most effective means, however, has proved to be word of mouth. One parishioner invites a nonmember whether churched or unchurched to visit his or her church. Some may advertise on the church page of the local newspaper.

Newer-paradigm ministries employ as many means of communication as are available and affordable. Some examples are direct mail, telemarketing, community service projects, a welcome wagon, America Online, media, special promotion Sundays, e-mail, door hangers, community prayer ministry, and word of mouth. They also use advertising but place their ads in other sections of the paper such as the sports page or the classified ads, as well as other sections that unchurched people read.

What Kind of Giving?

The pre-Boomer church passes the offering plate during both Sunday worship services and sometimes at the Wednesday evening prayer meeting. The pastor feels that he needs to preach and pressure people about tithing, especially if the church is running low on funds. People are naturally stingy, and they must be pressured to give more. The church posts each week's offerings somewhere in the sanctuary in plain view of the people as well as in the bulletin so that all can see the figures. There may be special fund drives where progress is measured by and displayed on a large cardboard thermometer that is placed up front in the sanctuary. People need to view giving as a part of their commitment to the church along with faithful (regular) attendance, whether the church is growing or dying. There is also a strong emphasis on giving money to missions overseas.

The younger-generation churches also pass the offering plate during the service, but probably not at every large group gathering. An occasional message on giving is appropriate, but most keep it low-key. Many of these churches use the small-group ministry to deal with financial needs and teach about giving. They have discovered that people tend to give to that which God is blessing and that which ministers to them. They respond best to significant visions, not constant, high-pressured statements of need.

What Kind of Care?

The professional pastoral staff in the typical ministry provides all or most of the pastoral care such as hospital and home visitation and counseling. In smaller churches this is the responsibility of the pastor. People love it when the pastor comes and sits with them on the front porch and sips a glass of ice tea or drinks a cup of hot coffee. Larger churches may have a minister of pastoral care who assumes these duties (often an older, retired pastor or a former senior pastor who has retired and remained in the community).

In the new-paradigm churches, lay pastors, small group leaders, lay persons with pastoral care gifts, and caring individuals provide most of the pastoral care in the context of a small group.

What Kind of Christian Education?

Most churches started before the 1960s provided a Sunday school program for children through adults and a nursery for infants. Most of the teachers followed a lecture format. Teacher training was often limited or nonexistent. In churches begun after the 1960s, children through adults will be in their own age-group/small-groups where teaching and other ministries take place. The teachers may be gifted, mature young people as well as gifted adults. They may use a lecture format but not exclusively. More likely, they will combine a number of different formats, such as questions and answers, debate, interviewing, drama, and so on. The small groups may involve themselves in seminars on discovering one's spiritual gifts, the spiritual life, witnessing, or other topics offered by the staff or some other specialists.

What Kind of Ministry?

People expect the pastoral staff of many traditional churches to do most of the work of the ministry, especially that requiring professional expertise such as preaching, visitation, ordinances, weddings, funerals, counseling, and other ministries. Lay persons are primarily responsible to attend services and tithe along with other minor voluntary functions as ushering, nursery duty, and so on.

The pastoral staff and others in less traditional ministries equip laity to do the work of the ministry, including services that are normally reserved for the ordained clergy. These may include preaching, teaching, the ordinances, weddings, funerals, counseling, and other ministries in the context of a small group ministry. Some go through a divine design seminar where they discover how God designed them. They discover and learn about their spiritual gifts, talents, abilities, passions, and temperaments.

What Kind of Special Services?

What distinguishes some churches from others are the special services that they provide outside their own religious programs that most non-Christians have come to expect from the church.

In the past, these services have been fairly generic in the typical church. In urban areas these include a soup kitchen, a shelter for battered women, a rescue mission, and other such services. These churches refer special needs to professionals such as medical doctors, psychologists, psychiatrists, and others. In more rural areas, several churches will often attempt to provide some of these special services for those in their community by means of a food pantry or support group program.

Many newer churches continue to provide the same services in the same way while a growing number of newer churches are attempting to provide some of these services in a more "tailored" approach. They are becoming more involved in helping out in the community. For example, some may help staff an inner-city school or work with special ministries or foundations that are helping poor people in the inner city. Some may have a psychologist or professional counselor on staff. A growing number of churches now provide small groups for people with special problems such as addictions, divorce recovery, victims of abuse, and so on. Some churches open up their facilities and invite the public to special events such as a 6K or 10K run, health fairs, divorce recovery workshops, and neighborhood crime watch programs. These often serve as "side door" events to the church that attract people who have felt that the church was not for them in the past.

What Kind of Facilities?

Pre-Boomers prefer that the facilities follow the typical architectural style of most older American churches. One reason is that for them the church is supposed to look "like a church." Its architecture distinguishes it from other buildings in the community. Another reason for their style preference is that certain building styles serve to bring back fond memories of a past church culture. For some it may be the small, white clapboard country church. For others it may be the brick church in the center of town with an imposing steeple. In their thinking, buildings should not only be attractive but also provide a certain measure of personal pride in the community.

Some churches that are in decline, however, may fail to note that their traditionally styled buildings are aging and in many cases in need of major repairs and remodeling. Older facilities often have inadequate sound systems and acoustics, difficult access for the handicapped (a concern, perhaps, of couples caring for older parents), and inadequate facilities for children.

Newer facilities are important especially if a church is targeting unchurched, professional people in urban or suburban North America. They expect quality, well planned facilities, and poorly maintained, aging structures will not attract them. It is also imperative that bathrooms and nursery facilities be well equipped and immaculate. For middle-class suburbanites, the old adage "Cleanliness is next to godliness" applies.

For this generation, it is more important that the facilities are functional than that they look like a church. Some congregations have begun to question the importance of traditional church architecture. Over the years, they have noted that a church's location is affected by changes in its community. As the community shifts and often declines, the church may need to relocate. It is easier to sell a facility that looks less like a church than one that is locked into a specific architectural pattern.

What Kind of Name?

The names of older churches may not be considered of particular importance to some Builders. However, a denominational affiliation such as Baptist, Episcopal, Methodist, and so on will be important to some although we are living in a postdenominational age. Builders may insist that the denominational label appear in the name of the church. As one elderly lady remarked: "We're proud that we're Methodists!" And another: "I was born a Baptist, and I'll die a Baptist. Why would I want to hide it?"

The choice of a name is very important to younger churches and may influence whether people in the target community will visit or join them. Names with the term *community* in them are popular. Denominational labels range anywhere from not important to a real turnoff for younger, unchurched people. One Boomer pastor in Washington State discovered that when his church removed the denominational label from its name, it began to reach the unchurched in the community.

What Kind of Atmosphere (Mood)?

Many traditional churches attempt to create an atmosphere that is quiet, reverent, and more formal. When parishioners enter the sanctuary, they should be quiet and reverent so all can pray and focus on God. If they have to talk or laugh, then they do so in the foyer or outside. Children may be seen but not heard in the worship services. The dress code is formal: The women wear dresses, and the men wear coats and ties. Little girls wear dresses and curl their hair; little boys may wear coats and ties with hair slicked down. Formality honors the Lord.

Today's more contemporary churches tend to be excited, expectant, and more casual. People may laugh and talk with one another even in the sanctuary. When they enter the facility, they are happy and expectant. They expect God to be present and to work in some special way in their lives during the service. They are excited about that prospect. Children may be in a service specially designed for them rather than the worship service. There is no dress code. Because seekers are present, people dress in a way that is most comfortable for them, ranging from three-piece suits to shorts but nothing that is distracting or immodest (2 Cor. 3:17; 1 Tim. 2:9–10).

A QUESTION

Usually the Builder generation prefers the older paradigm churches, and the Boomer and Buster generations opt for the new paradigm churches. One question is: What do you do if your present congregation has all three groups present, which is often the case in many established churches? Faith Chapel's congregation consists mostly of the Builder generation with a dwindling number of Boomer families mixed in. However, they hope to reach Boomers and Busters at their new location and be a multigenerational church. The answer is to provide for both in your forms or programs. This is called merging or blending.

Where a blended situation is most problematic is in the areas of worship, ministry expectations, and involvement in small group ministries. As stated above, it is difficult to combine a contemporary and a traditional worship format. If your church is large enough, it is best to plan two services—one contemporary and the other traditional. If it is a smaller church, then you might want to combine both styles in one service. However, this is not easy to accomplish, and you may alienate more people than you satisfy. If you attempt the latter, then seek out wise counsel from worship leaders in other churches in your community.

Different generations have different ministry expectations. Builders expect the pastor to visit them in the hospital and at home. If this does not occur, they feel slighted. However, this is next to impossible in a large church. Scripture is clear that pastors and other lay people are to train and equip the people to do the work of pastoral care (Eph. 4:11–12). However, in a blended situation, where the membership consists of Builders, Boomers, and even Busters, the pastoral staff may need to do some visitation and pastoral care with the elderly.

The pre-Boomer or Builder generation, in general, does not understand or accept the small group approach to ministry. Many of them prefer and are only comfortable with a more formal Sunday school approach. The solution is to provide both small group programs for Boomers and Busters alongside a Sunday school program for the Builders.

Whenever possible, attempt to structure the church's programs so that they minister to all the generations of people. In blended situations where you have to choose between the generations, it may be wise, though difficult and costly, to go with the younger people because they represent the future of your church. If you lose them, your church has no future.

CONCLUSION

Once you've thought through and answered the questions above, your strategy should be more obvious. Your decisions and answers to these questions will appear in the strategy statement that we will develop in the next chapter. As you work on the strategy, use common sense, creativity, and intuition as well. Follow the KISS principle (keep it simple, silly!).

Long-range planning is practically impossible considering the speed of change. Therefore, plan your strategy for three to five years but review it regularly—every six months to one year.

QUESTIONS FOR DISCUSSION AND REFLECTION

1. Name some churches that God is blessing overseas and in North America. How many could you name? If not many, why? What are they doing that the struggling churches are not doing? What can you learn from them that might help you in your strategy?

2. Name some of the church and parachurch ministries that God is blessing in your ministry community. How many could you name? If not many, why? What are they doing that might help your church? What can the Navigators teach you about discipleship? What can Campus Crusade teach you about evangelism?

3. Name some of the churches in your ministry area that are struggling. Why are they struggling? Do you know any of the pastors in these churches? What can you learn from them?

4. What generational groups are present in your church? How will their presence affect reaching your target group? Your target group consists primarily of which generation? If pre-Boomers or Builders are part of your church, then how will you minister to them and reach your target group at the same time?

5. If you have a significant number of pre-Boomers as well as Boomers or Busters in your ministry, what style of worship will you adopt? Will you attempt to implement more than one style of worship? If your answer is yes, will you attempt to implement more than one style in the same worship service? Why or why not?

6. A number of churches have discovered that some kind of small- or cell-group ministry is necessary to make disciples. Do you agree?

Why or why not? If you agree, then what will your small group program look like? If you have pre-Boomers, how will your program affect them?

7. Who is responsible for pastoral care in your church? If your answer is the pastoral staff, then are you satisfied with the amount and quality of care? Why or why not? If lay people are involved in pastoral care, are you satisfied with their performance? Why or why not? What can you or your church do to increase the amount and quality of the pastoral care?

ENDNOTES

1. Order from Dr. John Vaughn, Southwest Baptist Seminary, Bolivar, Missouri 65613.

2. Randy Frazee with Lyle Schaller, *Comeback Congregation* (Nashville: Abingdon Press, 1995), p. 11.

3. "Builders" is the term that Gary McIntosh uses in his excellent book *Three Generations* (Grand Rapids, Mich.: Fleming H. Revell, 1995).

4. Ibid., p. 173.

5. C. Peter Wagner, *Your Church Can Grow* (Ventura, Calif.: Regal Books, 1976), p. 120.

6. Carl F. George, *Prepare Your Church for the Future* (Tarrytown, N.Y.: Fleming H. Revell Company, 1991), p. 102.

CHAPTER EIGHT

The Plan for the Strategy

DEVELOPING A SET OF BLUEPRINTS

"All this," David said, "I have in writing from the hand of the LORD upon me, and he gave me understanding in all the details of the plan." —1 Chronicles 28:19

In several of their meetings with the congregation, Faith Chapel Church's board had announced that Pastor Robert Smith, with board input, would be the primary architect of the church's strategy for reaching their target group. They also announced that they would attempt to free up as much of his time as possible to devote to this project. This meant that the congregation would see less of him than they were accustomed. While he would continue to preach, they would hear an occasional guest speaker, and a board member or gifted lay leader might respond when someone went into the hospital or needed pastoral care.

Pastor Smith soon realized the board's wisdom. He discovered that he needed all the time he could find to work on the Chapel's strategy. To some degree, he had failed "to estimate the cost" (Luke 14:28) of the time that it would take to develop the document. Not only does developing a strategy itself take time, but listening to various phone calls and reading the stack of letters addressed to the pastor, all consisting of suggestions along with an occasional demand about the chapel's future direction, also proved to be time consuming.

As he attempted to develop the strategy, however, Pastor Robert soon realized that something vital was missing. He needed more than a mission statement and a strategy, as important and helpful as they are. He could not quite put his finger on what was missing, so, again, he retrieved his yellowed, coffee-stained seminary notes in an attempt to discover what he had overlooked. As he quickly scanned the material, he realized what was missing. The strategy does not exist by itself. Other vital elements are necessary to craft a significant strategy that will reach one's target community and minister to the existing church community. And those vital elements are all part of a larger strategic plan that one cannot put together overnight. Pastor Robert, like most pastors, knew that he needed to develop a strategic plan for his ministry. Few pastors, however, ever accomplish this because many don't realize the need for one nor do they know how to develop one if they did.

How will you implement your program to reach your target group? The answer is a plan. Scripture stresses the importance of planning (Luke 14:28–30; Prov. 15:22; 16:3–4). Not just any plan but a carefully thought through plan of which the strategy is a key part. You cannot have a strategy without a plan! A good plan consists of a statement of need, core values, mission, vision, a strategy, resources (personnel and budget), a schedule, and regular evaluation. The order here is important. This plan and its strategy assume that you have already developed a statement of values, mission, and vision because their development naturally precedes the strategy. Consequently, they will be included below but not developed extensively. The strategy is dependent on them and returns to and draws upon them for its formation and implementation.

Seminarians preparing for future ministry, church planters beginning ministry, and pastors involved in revitalization and renewal might question developing a full-blown plan and ultimately a ministry model when there is no way that they could implement such a plan so early in the ministry process or even in the immediate future. However, they must know where they are going from the beginning if they ever hope to get there. No one can focus on fog! A contractor begins the building process with a set of blueprints that provides him at the beginning with a picture of the finished project. The blueprints also guide the decisions that he and others will have to make along the way in the process of building a particular structure.

The ministry plan serves as the pastor's blueprints. By carefully thinking it through and writing it down, you also will know the end from the beginning. It will lay out the decisions you will need to make along the way and make it more likely that you will realize your dream. This chapter will help you develop your ministry blueprints and there is a sample plan in Appendix B. You may find it helpful to consult this plan as you read through this chapter. A simple ministry plan consists of the following: a statement of need, the values, mission, vision, strategy, resources, schedule, and evaluation (see fig. 8.1).

A Simple Ministry Plan
1. Need
2. Values
3. Mission
4. Vision
5. Strategy
6. Resources
7. Schedule
8. Evaluation

Figure 8.1

THE NEED

The strategic ministry plan opens with a statement of the community's need for the church. This statement explains or provides a rationale for its presence in the community and answers the question: Why is this church in this community? The need statement begins with a problem or better, a challenge, that the church faces such as a growing community consisting primarily of unchurched lost people or a community in decline. Then the rest of the document provides the solution. We all know the old aphorism "you can lead a horse to water but you can't make it drink." Your need statement is the salt that invites the reluctant horse (your church) to drink.

The information found in the need statement comes from the work you did in assessing your target group in chapter 6 and the internal and external audits in chapter 5. The statement ends with a brief, general description of your church (traditional, contemporary, relevant, or other) and how it will be the kind of church that can reach your target community. In chapter 6, I suggested that you construct a profile person that represents your target group. While the profile is communicated in sermons, brochures, and newcomers' classes, the need statement would also be an ideal place to present your profile person.

The statement of need can take several different formats. One is to present the information obtained in chapter 5 on the internal audit and the need to develop a disciple-making strategy or to improve the current strategy. The latter essentially says we are not as effective as we used to be; let us recoup and strategize (or restrategize) to move in a new direction. The following is an example of a need statement:

> Over the past ten years our neighborhood has changed dramatically. Many of our former neighbors have moved out to the suburbs and commute to work. God has brought to us our new neighbors who are primarily African American (60 percent) and Hispanic people (30 percent) in need of the Savior. However, because of cultural differences, they are used to and are attracted to a different style of worship than our own.
>
> This situation represents for us an exciting, new ministry challenge. There is a tremendous need for a high-impact, culturally relevant church to reach out to and win our new neighbors. We are convinced that we are that church. Therefore, we plan to do whatever it takes to become a church that is culturally relevant to our new neighbors to win them to Christ.[1]

Another format presents the demographic and psychographic information from chapter 6 on determining your target group. Place the information that you gathered from that chapter in this format. The following is an example that focuses on your ministry community:

> Our immediate community consists largely of a growing number of Baby Boomers and Baby Busters. They are highly educated and 89 percent are business and professional people. For the most part, they are unchurched (80 percent) and lost.
>
> Interviews indicate that they view the typical church as out of touch and not relevant to them and their needs (on average they attend church six times per year). Yet they are genuinely interested in spiritual truth. One survey found that 85 percent believe in the Bible, 94 percent pray regularly, 82 percent believe that Christ was God, and 75 percent believe in angels.
>
> All predictions indicate that our community will continue to experience unprecedented growth into the twenty-first century. Demographers project that two thousand people will move into this area in the next two to three years. However, there are few churches to reach them except for some older mainline denominations that are in sharp decline. At the same time the Mormons and Jehovah's Witnesses have targeted them and have been relatively successful as both have built new facilities within the last year.

Therefore, there exists a strong need for a culturally relevant church with a passionate desire to target and reach for the Savior these unchurched Boomers and Busters who currently are most interested in spiritual truth.

THE VALUES

One step toward a solution to the need represented in the above statement is the credo or values statement. Every ministry has certain basic core values. That may be good or bad. They are the constant, passionate, core beliefs that drive the ministry. They ask and answer the question: *Why* are we doing *what* we are doing? Your core values dictate every decision you make, every goal you set, your ministry forms, and every dime you spend. In short, they explain much of your church's behavior whether for good or bad. That is why they appear so early in the strategic plan.

You should know from the beginning what values are driving your ministry's vision and values statement. It is critical to the church or any ministry that it identifies its core values and places them in a credo or statement so that it knows and can articulate what drives it.

The following are three sample values that might appear in a credo or list of core values in a strategic ministry document.[2] They begin with a caption that quickly identifies the core value, a brief statement of the value with Scripture, and the term *therefore* signals how the value affects the ministry.

A Commitment to Creativity and Relevance

In today's rapidly changing world, we believe that our ministry methods are flexible, not our biblical principles (1 Cor. 9:19–23). Therefore, while maintaining our principles, we will regularly evaluate and change our forms of ministry to remain relevant to our times (1 Chron. 12:32).

A Commitment to Excellence

We believe that our God is a God of excellence who deserves the best we have to offer (1 Cor. 3:13). Therefore, in all our ministries and activities, we will seek to maintain the highest standards of excellence to the glory of God.

A Commitment to Growth

Although numerical growth is not a sufficient goal in itself, we believe that God wants us to reach as many people as possible with the gospel

(Matt. 28:19–20). Therefore, we will pursue methods that will facilitate numerical growth without compromising our integrity or commitment to biblical truth.

THE MISSION

Another step in the planning document that is part of a solution to the community's need is the church's mission statement. It represents the overall goal or direction of the church. The mission statement calls the ministry back to the basics. It asks the important, fundamental questions: What is the church all about? What is it supposed to be doing? What is the purpose of the church? The mission statement is key to the plan in general and the strategy in particular. The church's mission is what the strategy seeks to implement. A biblical mission statement is the Great Commission as found in Matthew 28:19–20, Mark 16:15, and other Scripture passages.

While the heart of the mission statement is the same, you may word it in slightly different ways that fit your church and its community. You should strive to keep it short. The vision statement will be longer than the mission statement and can be as long as a page in length. The mission statement should be concise and succinct. Peter Drucker states: "If you can get the mission statement on a T-shirt, then it is probably the appropriate length." Here are three examples:

Our mission is to honor our Lord and Savior, by intentionally pursuing the Great Commission (Mark 16:15). Therefore, we will do whatever it takes to pursue, win, and disciple the unchurched lost of this community.

Our comprehensive mission is the Great Commission (Matt. 28:19–20). In short, we are here to make disciples, to see God turn irreligious pagans into fully devoted disciples.

Our church's mission is to make completely committed Christians (Matt. 28:19–20).

THE VISION

Next is the vision statement. Vision is a "seeing" concept. Its use in planning is important but limited as compared to the mission statement. The mission statement is a planning tool while the vision statement functions more as a communication tool, a means of communicating the church's direction. Regardless, it should appear in the planning document and is a fuller development of the shorter mission statement. The latter is brief and to the point and will dictate the goals that make up the strategy. The former creates a picture or snapshot of what the mission statement will look like as it is realized in the church's community. The following is a sample of what a shorter vision statement might look like.[3]

> We envision reaching those in this city and the surrounding area who do not regularly attend any church. To accomplish this, our church will be an equipping center that will develop every Christian to his or her full potential for ministry. As a result, our city will be different in ten to fifteen years, with a Christian influence being felt in homes, businesses, education, and politics. We further intend to multiply our worldwide ministry by planting churches, preparing our people for leadership roles in vocational ministries and parachurch groups, sending out missionaries, and becoming a resource center and model for this state and the nation.

It is best to identify and articulate your vision and core values before attempting to develop the strategy. The reality, however, is that you, like Pastor Robert Smith, may be pressed for time. You could be facing a board-mandated deadline. In this case, you may delay the vision and values development, but not the mission statement. It is vital to the strategy, and you must develop it before you attempt the strategy.

THE STRATEGY

Once the church has articulated a statement of need, its values, mission, and vision, then it has answered the critical questions of why it is located in the community, why it does what it does, what it is supposed to be doing, and what that looks like when it is realized in the target community. Now it is ready to craft a tailor-made strategy that will answer the question: How will we accomplish the mission? That is: How will we accomplish the church's mission as articulated in the mission statement and visualized for us in our vision statement? Much of the rest of this chapter covers the development of your strategy.

Since the strategy is what this book is all about, this section will be much larger and more developed than any other part of the plan. Church planters will find that this section will help them to develop the future strategy of their church. Pastors leading churches through renewal and revitalization can use this information to both critique their present strategy and develop a new strategy for the future. As you work your way through the information in this chapter, you may want to consult the model strategy that I have provided as an example in the next chapter.

Articulate the Mission Statement

The first step in developing the strategy is to articulate the mission statement that you developed earlier in this ministry plan. Again, it is a planning tool that is key to the development of the strategy. If the strategy accomplishes the mission statement, then the first step in developing the strategy is to return to and begin with the mission statement.

The mission statement is the general, overall goal of the church. It asks: *What* are we supposed to be doing? The answer is the Great Commission: "Therefore, go and make disciples . . ." (Matt. 28:19–20; Mark 16:15; Acts 1:8).

The church's mission is developing completely committed Christians (fully devoted followers of Christ). Note the shortness of the mission statement. Short statements are clear and easily remembered.

Making disciples is a process that moves people from prebirth to maturity, that is, it moves them from wherever they are along their spiritual journey (saved or unsaved) to where God wants them to be (maturity). Disciple making is imperative for the church of Jesus Christ. If we do not make disciples, our new believers will sink into the quicksand of nominal Christianity. Matthew 7:26–27 and 13:20–22 seem to indicate that the repercussions of not making disciples could be even worse than nominal Christianity. New believers may collapse like a house built on sand in a devastating storm ("and it fell with a great crash"), or they may drop out ("fall away") all together.

After you have reviewed the mission statement and its critical role in relation to the strategy, break down the mission (the overall goal) into specific goals (at least two and no more than six or seven) that will accomplish or realize the mission. These major goals are not just any goals but summarize the natural progression, steps, or levels of commitment that your people will move through to achieve their personal mission and the church's corporate mission of becoming Christ's disciples. For example:

The Mission (Overall Goal) of Our Church

Our comprehensive mission is to make fully devoted disciples (Matt. 28:19–20) of those living in our targeted community (Acts 1:8).

The major goals that will accomplish this mission:

Goal #1: To interest our target group in becoming a disciple.
          To lead our group to Christ and active involvement in our church.
Goal #2: To become a growing disciple.
          To grow people to spiritual maturity.
Goal #3: To become a serving disciple.
          To equip people for and involve them in ministry both within and outside the body of believers.
Goal #4: To become a disciple maker.
          To enlist disciples for leadership locally and in the world.

These goals are critical because you will both hire staff and budget to meet each goal; that is, you will need a leader (a gifted lay leader or staff person) and line items in your budget (your budget should be built around each goal) to implement each major goal. It is important that these goals be kept in balance so that you emphasize each one equally. The temptation will be to major on one and ignore the others, depending on your gifts and abilities. If you succumb to this temptation, you will risk becoming a single-trait, imbalanced church that does not make disciples. Staffing and budgeting around each major goal will help you to avoid this. I will say more about the problem later in the chapter.

Determine What a Disciple Looks Like

The second step in developing the strategy is to determine what a fully devoted disciple (the mission of the church) looks like. Before you can go any further, you must envision your mission statement. Here it is helpful to return to the concept of vision as a *seeing* concept. While this is not the process for developing the vision statement as above, it is similar. In developing a strategy, it asks: What does maturity *look like*? What does a disciple or a completely committed Christian or a fully devoted follower *look like*? How would you know one if you *saw* him or her? The answer or solution is to develop specific, *observable* behavior traits of a disciple. By taking this step, you keep your mission statement from becoming too broad, vague, and unmeasureable.

A Theology of Discipleship

To develop observable behavior traits, you will need to develop a theology of discipleship. This will involve you in a personal study of the biblical teaching on discipleship. Start with passages in the Gospels and Acts that use the term *disciple* (Matt. 16:24–27; 28:19–20; Mark 8:34–38; Luke 9:23–26; 14:25–35; John 8:31; 13:34–35; 15:7–17). Another word that speaks of discipleship in the New Testament is "follow" and a parallel term is *to come after* (Matt. 16:24; Luke 9:23). Include other passages from the epistles that also apply to discipleship even though the term is used only in the Gospels and Acts.

Matthew 28:19–20 teaches that making disciples involves not only baptism but obedience to Jesus' commands. Jesus' primary interest in disciple making was not merely to impart information as so many of our schools and seminaries are doing, but to awaken a full, passionate commitment to him that produces fruit. Cognitive input is insufficient by itself; character formation is essential. Our world does not hunger for more highly educated Christians; it hungers for a greater number of completely devoted disciples.

What do committed disciples look like? Mature, fully devoted disciples will look like Jesus (Gal. 4:19; 5:22–23). They will be more than just knowledgeable Christians; they will be godly Christians. Those who would be Christ's disciples must also understand that discipleship is more than having your devotions along with a cup of coffee in the morning. That is safe. In the first century, Christ's disciples literally died for him. Those who did not suffer physical death did die for him in a spiritual sense (Matt. 16:24–25).

At issue is the meaning of the command "make disciples" (Matt. 28:19–20), which is the mission of the church. Does it mean evangelism, evangelism only, or does it include more than that? I believe Scripture teaches that discipleship is a process that can begin before conversion (what I refer to as spiritual prebirth) but usually begins at conversion and moves to a deep commitment to Christ (maturity). Therefore, discipleship involves the process of moving from spiritual prebirth to maturity. The New Testament concurs and uses the term *disciple* in three ways.

First, an unbeliever can be a disciple according to a strict definition of the term (a pupil, apprentice, adherent, learner). Consequently, if unbelievers want to learn about Christ, then in a sense they are disciples. This was true of the crowd in John 6:60–67. They listened to Jesus' words, and John calls them disciples in verse 60. However, Jesus says that some did not believe, and that his words offended them (vv. 60, 64). Thus in time many turned back and stopped following him (v. 66). A seeker would fall into this category. Dwight Pentecost calls these unbelieving disciples the *curious*.[4]

Second, a disciple is one who is saved but not necessarily deeply or completely committed to Christ. In John 12:42–43, John notes that many of the Jewish leaders believed in Jesus. However, they would not confess their newfound faith for two reasons. They feared the reaction of the Pharisees who would put these new believers out of the synagogue, and they loved the praise of men more than the praise of God. Later, the text identifies Joseph of Arimathea as a secret disciple who also feared the Jews (John 19:38). Pentecost calls these disciples the *convinced*.[5]

Third, a disciple is one who is saved and ranges anywhere from committed to deeply committed. Pentecost appropriately calls them the *committed*.[6] Some characteristics of committed disciples are the following:

1. They deny themselves, take up their cross, and follow Christ. In other words, they are willing to lose their lives for Christ's sake: Matthew 16:24–27; Mark 8:34–38; Luke 9:23–26; Acts 2:45; 4:32–35.
2. They put Christ ahead of their families or love Christ more than their families. Scripture says that they must hate their own father and mother, spouse and children, brothers and sisters, even their own lives (carrying your own cross): Matthew 10:37; Luke 14:25–35. The use of the term *hate* here is problematic in North American culture. The term is a Semitic figure of speech or way of speaking that means to love less. The idea is that they must love and commit to Jesus more than to their families.
3. They abide in Christ's word or follow his teachings: John 8:31; Acts 2:42.
4. They love other disciples as Christ loves them: John 13:34–35; 15:11–17; Acts 2:42; 4:32.
5. They bear fruit: John 15:7–17.
6. They have been baptized: Matthew 28:19.
7. They are obedient to Christ's commands: Matthew 28:20; John 15:9–10.
8. Other characteristics may be found in other books and epistles of the New Testament although the term *disciple* is not used there.

Becoming Christ's disciples is an exciting venture of faith although it is anything but easy. Regardless, Christ calls us to come and join him, patiently work through the many obstacles that stand in our way, and be one of his committed disciples.

How Various Churches Describe a Disciple

Different churches have different answers to the question "What does a disciple look like?" You will find it helpful and instructive to be aware of these. The following are some common answers:

1. The legalistic church: Committed Christians are marked by what they do not do. For example, they do not use tobacco (smoke, dip, or chew), drink alcoholic beverages, go to movies, participate in dancing, or associate with people who do (five traits).
2. The teaching church: Mature Christians are knowledgeable Christians, specifically, those who know their Bibles well (one primary trait).
3. The evangelistic church: Christ's disciples are those who share their faith on a regular basis and see people come to faith (one primary trait).
4. The social conscience church: Mature Christians are those who are actively involved in a cause such as the family, the prolife/ anti-abortion movement, traditional moral values, home schools, civil rights, justice, gender or racial equality, and other causes. (The one primary trait is that a disciple is involved in a *cause*.)
5. The charismatic church: A committed disciple is one who is anointed by the Spirit and experiences wondrous things such as the baptism of the Spirit, tongues, healing, and other miracles (several traits).
6. The family reunion church: Mature Christians are those who are faithful to the church. Faithfulness is defined as regularly attending the Sunday morning service, tithing, and showing up on church work days (primarily three traits).

These churches exhibit many traits. Some are biblical, such as the teaching and evangelistic churches. Some are not so biblical, as the legalistic church that has sidetracked and turned off numerous Christians since the first century. Some are helpful and some are harmful while others fall short, such as the family reunion church. One important feature that they all have in common is that each lacks balance. Using the Great Commission as Christ's mission for the church, the teaching church comes up short in evangelism, and the evangelistic church comes up short in teaching. Other churches overlook such important areas as teaching, evangelism, and worship altogether.

A Balanced, Biblical Perspective

Contrary to the above examples, a more balanced and biblical answer to the question "What does a disciple look like?" exists. After they have developed a biblical theology of discipleship, churches must determine what a disciple looks like for their own ministries. Here is one example of the behavioral traits of balanced, mature Christians:

Trait #1: They have a growing knowledge of the Bible and basic theology and are intentionally applying it to their lives (they are "hearers and doers" of the Word).

Trait #2: They spend regular devotional time (worship, prayer, and Bible study) with God and instill this value in their families.

Trait #3: They are regular attendees of church and actively participate in a small group.

Trait #4: They understand their gifts and are involved in one or more area(s) of ministry according to their gifts and abilities.

Trait #5: They are building relationships with the lost, sharing Christ and inviting them to a service relevant to them.

Trait #6: They are generous, joyful givers of their God-given resources (time, talents, and treasure).

Having determined what a disciple looks like, the important question becomes: What will it take to produce someone like this? The ones who are crafting the strategy and their teams should ask this question of each trait. The rest of this chapter will answer the question.

Finally, it is important to note that by developing a mission and strategy for your ministry, you eliminate guessing at your ministry's future. To a certain extent, you will know what that future looks like. The mission statement is your preferred future. The strategy is a matter of determining how best to get there.

Determine the Steps Necessary to Make a Disciple

The third step in developing a strategy is to determine the number of steps or stages necessary to make a disciple. The strategy might consist of two, three, four, or more steps that are necessary to produce fully devoted disciples. Each represents an increasing level of commitment from the disciple. Therefore, you may want to refer to these steps as levels (Level 1, Level 2, and so forth) as I have done in the sample in the next chapter. These steps, stages, or levels of commitment provide a structure upon which you construct the strategy. The strategy is analogous to muscles, and the structure to the bones that support the muscles. First you decide on the number of steps, and second, you identify each. The key to knowing the number of steps or levels is the number of major goals that you developed earlier in this chapter to accomplish the overall mission statement. The number of goals will equal the number of levels because each level has a corresponding goal associated with it.

Most see Christ's discipleship process as consisting of three to four phases. In the *Disciple Making Pastor*, Bill Hull believes that Christ discipled around four phases: "come and see," "come and follow me," "come and be with me," and "you will remain in me."[7] A. B. Bruce's *The Training of the Twelve* presents three phases. Willow Creek Community Church has seven steps in its disciple-making strategy. No biblical imperative exists that predetermines or dictates the number of levels or steps your church must have. The exact number is up to you. However, too many can be confusing.

After you choose the number of steps that it will take to develop a disciple, next you will need to identify each step in the strategy. Be succinct and attempt to capture the essence of each level. The following is one example:

Level 1: Interesting in Christ
Level 2: Growing in Christ
Level 3: Ministering in Christ
Level 4: Leading in Christ

Attempt to be creative in identifying each level. For example, you could depict these levels as Rick Warren does using base paths.

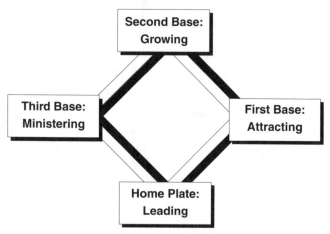

The battles that make up our spiritual war with Satan may be a helpful analogy (the term *strategy* is military in its origin). The following says that there are three battles we must win if we are to be Christ's disciples or warriors, and a fourth if we are to make spiritual warriors:

> Battle #1: To interest in becoming a warrior
> Battle #2: To become a growing warrior
> Battle #3: To become a serving warrior
> Battle #4: To become a warrior maker

Another example uses the apple. It starts on the outside with the skin and moves to the middle or the apple core.

> The Skin: Attracting
> The Meat: Growing and ministering
> The Core: Leading

Like the profile-person concept in chapter 6 (Duncanville Dan, Saddleback Sam, and others), these strategy concepts create a mental picture of the strategy that your people will never forget. Thus, it will serve to answer the question: What is the simplest, most powerful, most memorable way to communicate our strategy to our congregation? The only limit on what you can develop is your creativity.

Match Each Level with Its Goal

The fourth step in developing the strategy is to match your major goals with the levels of commitment. Each level will have a corresponding goal. Actually, you have already determined these goals when you developed the major goals from the overall mission statement earlier in this chapter (see p. 143). One of those major goals will fit under each level. Here is an example.

> Level 1: Interesting in Christ

> Goal: To lead people to Christ and active involvement in the church (to interest in *becoming* a disciple)

You should make sure that the goals are sequential so that there is a logical or chronological flow, that is, one builds on another. (You may see an example of this flow in the sample in the next chapter.) This is most important because it provides the ministry with a sense of momentum. It is critical that people see themselves as moving or making progress in the faith.

Develop Action Steps

The fifth step is to develop action steps. Every goal must have an action step that accomplishes the goal. Other terms for action steps are *method, objective,* or *vehicle.* Developing the action steps for each goal involves thinking through several areas such as the source, traits, age groups, time, and even a diagram for the strategy.

The Source

Much of the information that makes up your strategy will come from the program step in chapter 7 that answers the question: What kind of church will it take to reach our target group? It focuses on such things as what kind of meetings, worship, teaching, evangelism, and so on that you will implement in your church. Consequently, you have already made most of the necessary decisions for the strategy and determined the general programs. This is the place where they fit with your strategy. The sample strategy document in the next chapter shows how this all works together.

The Behavioral Traits

In designing the strategy for your ministry, you will need to take into account the behavioral traits of a disciple that you list as the result of taking the second step above. Here is where you place that information. Ask: How and where does the strategy accomplish each trait? A helpful check is to note in parentheses after the strategy statement which trait the strategy accomplishes. I would suggest that you put the trait in bold type for quick recognition as I have done in the sample in chapter 7.

Age Groups

You must also consider how you plan to disciple the various age groups in your church. A part of our mission is to disciple all of our people, including young people. Will you have an age-graded Sunday school or a learning center? Will the children, teens, and adults be in small groups? Will young people have their own large group meetings?

Time

Determine approximately how much time you think it will take to accomplish each level or step. In other words, how long should it take or will it take to move someone through each level? What is a reasonable time span for each? What should be your expectations and their expectations so that both of you can judge progress? Lee Strobel, a pastor at Willow Creek Community Church, states that he spent two years as a seeker before coming to faith in Christ. Is two years short, long, or typical for a seeker in your community? What should you expect? Can or should you be flexible?

Diagram

Devise a diagram that communicates the entire strategy (all the levels of commitment) to your people. This will help them to easily remember it and keep track of where they have been, where they are, and where they need to go in their growth. Again, it is important to come up with creative ways whether in a diagram or some other form to communicate all the levels of commitment or steps of discipleship to your people. Review the examples above—Rick Warren's baseball diamond diagram, an apple, and spiritual battles—and see what creative variations or alternatives you can come up with.

THE RESOURCES

The resources are twofold, consisting of the ministry personnel and the ministry budget. The first is the personnel.

Personnel

The key to selecting and placing ministry personnel is to staff to your goals. A goal should be under each step or level of the strategy. You would be wise to look for the right servant whether a gifted lay person or staff person (such as a minister of involvement) to lead each level of the strategy and accomplish its goal. This means that you look for someone (lay person or professional) who is uniquely designed (gifts, passion, temperament) to lead at that level. In church planting or a smaller church, this will be a gifted lay leader. These people will surface at levels 3 and 4 where they discover and develop their gifts and are trained for leadership.

As a leader, it becomes this person's job to build a team to minister at each level. (I believe that New Testament ministry is team ministry.) The team is responsible to plan and execute the programs for each level.

Initially, the pastor may be the staff leader for each goal, especially when the church is small. However, he must quickly find the right person to replace him. This fits with his role as a coach and developer of leaders. Ultimately, his role is to oversee and coach the leaders of all levels (Exod. 18:13–27). Since most pastors tend to be gifted in and emphasize one particular area over another (preaching, evangelism, and so forth), the concept of staffing at each level promotes and maintains a more balanced ministry.

Budget

Not only do leaders staff at each level but they budget at each level as well. You should design the entire budget around each ministry level that has its own line items. (See the sample budget in Appendix A.) Therefore, the leader and team at each level are responsible to develop a budget for their ministries.

Funding might come from one primary source such as a large group offering or each phase might be responsible to raise its own funding. For example, the small groups might take an offering as a part of their worship. This again insures a more balanced approach to the ministry.

THE SCHEDULE

When will the various ministries and meetings take place? When will the large group meetings occur? The answers to these questions have everything to do with a group's purpose along with issues such as when the target group will come to a large group service.

Small groups can meet at the discretion of those who make up the group. They could meet three times a month, taking off one week when the leader and apprentice leaders meet together for leadership training. They also have the option of taking the summer off.

This process does not happen overnight. It takes time to develop a discipleship program for a church. The problem, however, is that the average pastor lasts 3.7 years which is not enough time to become a leader or implement a strategy. I address this problem in my book *Values-Driven Leadership.*[8]

THE EVALUATION

Regular ministry evaluation is essential to any ministry if it is to improve and serve its membership (Prov. 15:22). My experience is that few churches do any kind of evaluation except when the people randomly evaluate the pastor's sermon over lunch every Sunday!

It is important that those who lead and serve in ministry regularly evaluate their ministries. They should constantly ask: How can we do it better next time? They might invite others to evaluate them as well. This will result in incremental change and ministry excellence. With this approach, change comes from the grass roots up by those who are actually doing the ministry rather than vice versa. (This is by far the best way to initiate and implement change.)

Every program has a shelf life. It is wise to drop those programs that have outlived theirs and are obsolete. Otherwise, you are adding new layers of paint on top of peeling, existing layers. Eventually, the bottom peels loose and it affects the entire finish.

QUESTIONS FOR DISCUSSION AND REFLECTION

1. Does it make sense to develop a full-blown ministry plan, including a strategy, when there is no way to implement the entire plan right now or in the immediate future? Why or why not? How is this process similar to a contractor using a set of blueprints to construct a building?

2. Why is your church in your community? In light of what your ministry is accomplishing, is there a need for it in the community? What is it? How important are your core values to the ministry? What are your core values? Why do the ministry's core values come so early in the planning process?

3. What are some of the differences between a vision statement and a mission statement? Has your church developed either one? If it has, can you articulate them? Which is more important to the development of your strategy? Why? What is the relationship of the strategy to the mission statement?

4. The development of a strategy involves breaking the mission statement (the overall goal) into several major goals. What are some major goals that come to mind for your church? How do they relate to disciple making?

5. What does the Bible mean when it commands us to make disciples? Does it include evangelism, evangelism only, or other functions? Over the past years, what have been the acceptable traits of a disciple in your church? Are they biblical? Are they balanced? Have you developed a theology of discipleship? Why or why not? As you think about what a biblical disciple should look like, what are some traits that might characterize your church's disciples?

6. How many steps or levels do you believe are necessary to become a fully committed disciple? According to this chapter, what are some creative ways to illustrate the various levels of commitment

in your strategy for disciple making? Initially, are you attracted to any one of these in particular? If yes, which one? If no, why not? What are some creative illustrations that are not mentioned in this chapter?

7. In general, how does your ministry presently handle its personnel and budget? What is the basis for selecting and assigning ministry personnel? How do you determine where you deploy your finances? How would implementing a disciple-making strategy affect the present handling of your ministry's resources? What might change? What would remain the same?

8. Does any evaluation presently take place in your ministry? If yes, what? If no, why not? How open are the people in your ministry to evaluation and change? Do they prefer change "from on high" or do they prefer to initiate change themselves (change from the grass roots up)?

ENDNOTES

1. While this sounds good and I would encourage some to try it, it is doubtful that the typical congregation can make this kind of transition. Instead, many, like Faith Chapel, sell or give their facilities to a church in the area that is already ministering to the new community. Other churches move out of the area and continue to minister to their constituency in a new community.

2. For more information about this process, see Aubrey Malphurs, *Vision-Driven Leadership* (Grand Rapids, Mich.: Baker Book House, 1996). I wrote this book to help leaders identify their core values and those of their ministries and then draft a credo that articulates those values.

3. For more on the vision and how to develop one for your church, see Aubrey Malphurs, *Developing a Vision for Ministry in the 21st Century* (Grand Rapids, Mich.: Baker Book House, 1992).

4. J. Dwight Pentecost, *Design for Discipleship* (Grand Rapids, Mich.: Kregel Publications, 1996), p. 14.

5. Ibid., p. 17.

6. Ibid.

7. Bill Hull, *The Disciple Making Pastor* (Old Tappan, N.J.: Fleming H. Revell, 1988), p. 214.

8. Aubrey Malphurs, *Values-Driven Leadership* (Grand Rapids, Mich.: Baker Book House, 1996).

PART THREE

The Product
of Developing a Strategy

The result of working through the strategy process is a strategy product—your initial ministry strategy. Part 3 consists of two chapters. Chapter 9 will present several sample strategies as a guide to what an initial strategy might look like. Chapter 10 provides some strategies that various church and parachurch ministries have constructed to move their people from prebirth to maturity. They are included to catalyze and prompt your thinking.

CHAPTER NINE

A Sample Strategy for Making Disciples

HERE'S HELP!

"Listen now to me and I will give you some advice, and may God be with you." —Exodus 18:19

About once a week, Pastor Robert Smith wakes up in the middle of the night in a cold sweat. When this occurs, he usually gets out of bed, drinks a glass of water, prays for half an hour, and then attempts to go back to sleep. Sometimes it works. Other times, he cannot fall back asleep, so he gets dressed and drives to the church to commence what will be a long day at the office. He has found, however, that these have been some of his most creative and productive days. Regardless, his wife is quietly concerned. She does not say much to him, but inwardly she worries that he might develop a heart condition, as did his dad, who died prematurely of a heart attack.

Pastor Robert knows what is wrong. It is all the stress he is feeling, and much of it is self-imposed. The problem is twofold. First, he is under a board-mandated deadline to develop the church's strategy, and he is behind. Second, he realizes that to a certain degree, the future of the church rests in his ability to craft a strategy that is tailor-made for the Chapel and then to persuade the people to adopt and implement it. On the one hand, he is frightened as he has never been before. On the other, he is convinced that God is in this and will give him the wisdom and strength to pull it off.

Actually, the end is in sight, and he notes that his early-hour episodes have begun to occur less frequently, if not cease all together. Even though he is still behind the board's deadline, he has completed two-thirds of the strategy and feels good about what he has developed thus far, though he has no sample to guide him. He had relied totally on his seminary notes that, back then, were considered cutting edge but contained no samples of what a strategy looked like. However, an occasional meeting over coffee with his seminary professor, who has agreed to serve as a part-time consultant on these matters, made the difference. Having worked with other churches in strategy development, he provided Robert with a sample strategy as a guide.

What might a completed strategy look like? What is a potential product of the process? This chapter consists of a sample strategy that a consultant such as Robert's former professor might use with a church and its leadership in crafting a disciple-making strategy. It is a sample for a new paradigm ministry and would not serve as an exact model for a more traditional church like Faith Chapel. Nevertheless, it should prove helpful to anyone leading a church through the strategizing process. While the process is the key, a model or product helps immensely in the process. The following model consists of an intentional disciple-making mission and strategy and includes some questions you must ask in crafting your strategy. I have placed two other sample strategies in the appendixes (C and D). You may find it helpful to consult them as you read through this chapter.

THE MISSION OF THE CHURCH
(THE OVERALL GOAL)

The mission of the church asks: What are we supposed to be doing?

The answer is the Great Commission: "to make disciples" or "to make fully devoted disciples" (Matt. 28:19–20; Mark 16:15; Luke 24:47; Acts 1:8).

This is a disciple-driven mission! Therefore, the mission of this church is to make completely committed Christians.

The specific goals (to realize the mission):
  #1. To lead people to Christ and active involvement in our church (to interest in *becoming* a disciple)
  #2. To grow people to spiritual maturity (to become a *growing* disciple)
  #3. To equip for and involve people in ministry both within and outside the body of believers (to grow into a *serving* disciple)
  #4. To enlist disciples for leadership locally and in the world (to serve in discipling others)

THE TRAITS OF A DISCIPLE

What does a fully devoted disciple look like? How would you know one if you saw him or her? What should we look for? The following are some biblical, measurable behavioral traits or characteristics of an authentic disciple:

Trait #1. A basic, growing knowledge of the Bible and applies it to his or her life (John 8:31–32)

We will help the disciple to understand how the Bible is organized into the Old and New Testament and the general contents of each. You will know where to go for wisdom (Proverbs, James), worship (Psalms), etc. You will also gain a knowledge of basic Bible study skills. We will coach you to regularly ask the question: So what? What difference will this biblical truth make in my life, marriage, work, etc. today, tomorrow, next year?

Trait #2. A regular devotional time (prayer, worship, etc.) with God and the family (John 15:7–8)

We will coach and encourage you to spend regular devotional time individually and with your family. We will instruct you in the various ways to accomplish this, and you will see it modeled in the lives and families of others.

Trait #3. A daily recommitment (putting the Savior first) of one's life to Christ (Luke 9:23–25; 14:25–35)

We will encourage and exhort you to make a total commitment of your life to Christ as one of your most important life decisions. In addition, we will supply encouragement and accountability so that you might follow this up with a weekly or better a daily recommitment of yourself and all that you own to Him (Rom. 6–8; 12:1–2).

Trait #4. Regular attendance at church and membership in a small group (Heb. 10:25; John 13:34–35;15:7–17; Acts 2:46; 5:42; 8:3; 20:20)

We have designed our large group meetings to address the relevant issues of our daily lives from the Scriptures as we worship God together.

We are not a church with small groups but a church of small groups. Therefore, we also request that you become a vital part of one of our vibrant small groups where much of our discipleship itself takes place.

Trait #5. Understands his or her gifts and is involved in a ministry (1 Tim. 4:14; 2 Tim. 1:6; Eph. 4:11–13)

God has wonderfully designed all of us in a unique way to serve him. He has called and gifted us to be his servants whether within or outside the four walls of the church. It is our goal to help you discover who you are, like who you are, and be who you are while serving the Savior.

Trait #6. Building relationships and sharing the faith ("a fisher of men") with lost people at home and abroad (Matt. 9:36–38)

Because lost people matter to God, they matter to us (Luke 15; 19:1–10). We desire to do whatever it takes to help you reach the toughest mission field of your life—your neighbors, family, and workmates.

Trait #7. A generous, joyful giver (2 Cor. 8)

All that we possess is a gracious gift from God that ultimately belongs to Him. Therefore, we will provide you with instruction on biblical giving and encourage you to invest in God's work throughout this ministry.

Note: These traits are found below in parentheses next to the objective(s) that accomplish(es) them.

STRATEGY

The following strategy is how we move people from prebirth to maturity. It consists of four levels. The term *level* implies level of commitment. The range is from level 1 (the least amount of commitment) up to level 4 (the maximum amount of commitment).

Note: When a person reaches level 3, he or she is realizing the mission. While level 4 is not necessary for one to be a completely committed disciple, every church must develop leaders who are disciple-makers.

Level 1: Interesting in Christ
Goal

- To lead people to Christ and active involvement in the church (to interest in becoming a disciple) (Luke 15:1–10; 19:1–10; Col. 4:2–6; 2 Tim. 4:4; 1 Cor. 14:22–25)
- To call unchurched lost and saved people (young people as well as adults) out of the stands (inactivity) and onto the playing field (serious, authentic Christian service).

Strategy

1. A seeker-friendly large group meeting to interest lost and saved young people and adults in becoming disciples. This is a "front door" event.

   A. Sermon—mostly topical that teaches biblical truth and shows its relevancy to everyday life
   B. Drama—short, relevant accounts that set up or introduce the sermon topic and/or make application to life
   C. Worship—contemporary, celebrative music led by a praise band
   D. Prayer—a time of public prayer for the world, nation, and community
   E. Evangelism—a regular presentation of the gospel through sermons, drama, and other events

2. A small group to lead people to Christ and/or orient them to the church (its expectations, beliefs, programs, etc.). It loves and cares for them as well. These groups are in the early stages of initiating the disciple-making process. They are explaining what the church is all about and inviting those in the group to move on with Christ. Those who stick with the group go on to phase 2 (Trait #4).

   A. Basic small groups for people.
      These are communities that minister to all ages from children's groups to older adult groups. (The small group approach will replace the traditional Sunday school for our children and young people.) The ordinances (Lord's Supper and baptism) will take place in this context.
   B. Special small groups for special people.
      Twelve-step Groups, Addiction Groups, Abuse Groups, Women's and Men's Groups, Premarriage Groups, Divorce Recovery Groups, and so forth.

3. Other events (to minister to people and hold them in the church). vacation Bible school, aerobics, choir, children's clubs, sports events, and others.

Time

How long should a person be at level 1? Six months? One to two years? (Pastor Lee Strobel of Willow Creek Community Church needed two years.)

Note: Both the large- and small-group leaders constantly invite these people to become fully devoted disciples, that is, to move to level 2.

Level 2: Growing in Christ
Goal
- To grow people to spiritual maturity (to become a *growing* disciple) (Col. 1:28; Eph. 4:12-13; 1 Tim. 4:7-8; Heb. 6:1-3)

Strategy—Discipleship Small Groups
(fully functioning communities)

Lay pastor-leaders will be responsible to equip the people in their small groups directly or through a seminar given by a specialist in our church in each of the following key areas that are essential to becoming a disciple:
1. Scripture—to gain a knowledge of the Bible, theology, and how to study the Bible on one's own (Trait #1)
2. Prayer—to learn about and practice private and public prayer (Trait #2)
3. Worship—to learn how to worship and to practice private and public worship (Trait #2)
4. Evangelism—to discover one's evangelism style and begin to share the gospel with the lost in his or her relational group, community, and the world (missions) (Trait #6)
5. Giving—to learn about and practice biblical giving (Trait #7)
6. Commitment—to learn the importance of and commit to attending the meetings of the church; more important to commit one's life to the Lord daily (Traits # 3 & #4)

Time

One to two years?

Level 3: Ministering in Christ
Goal

- To equip people for and involve them in ministry (to become a *serving* disciple) (Eph. 4:11–12; 1 Cor. 12:12–31; Rom. 12:1–8; 1 Tim. 4:14)

This lay mobilization primarily involves helping people to discover their gifts, direction, and ministry placement so that they can become Christ's servants (servanthood). This phase provides the committed workers whose ministry may take place within the four walls of the church or outside in the local communityæinner-city mission, church planting, and so on.

Strategy

1. The person will continue in his/her discipleship small group while at this level and after he or she has completed it. Disciples thrive on community and will always need one another (see all the "one another" passages in the New Testament).
2. A staff or lay minister of involvement will visit the group for several weeks and take them through the Lay Mobilization process (Trait #5).
3. A staff or lay minister of involvement will match the disciples with the church's ministries for which they are best suited according to their design. If there is no existing match, they may start a new ministry. However, we will start no ministries without a leader. Those in the current ministry are responsible to train the disciple recruit. The disciple as Christ's servant will continue to minister within or outside the church for the duration of his or her time at the church and hopefully the rest of his or her life.

Time

One to three months?

Level 4: Leading in Christ
Goal

- To enlist disciples as lay and professional leaders of ministries at home and abroad (to become disciple makers) (1 Tim. 3:1–13; Titus 1:1–9; Acts 6:1–7; 2 Tim. 2:2)

This is the all-important leadership development phase. It is where you equip and develop the gifted men and women who will become small-group leaders, deacons, elders, church staff, church planters, and missionaries of the church (Trait #6). Therefore, you as a pastor and staff will pour much of your time into this stage and these critical people. Note that this is a process and no one becomes a leader overnight (the "warm body" approach)! Interns from seminaries, Bible colleges, and Christian schools will do their internships in this phase.

> Note: Not everyone who is a disciple is expected to move to level 4. This is for a select, gifted group who are key to the ministry. The staff and small group leaders in particular look for these gifted leaders (including mature teenagers) and individually invite and encourage them to consider moving on to level 4.

Strategy
1. The prospective leader must meet certain requirements for leadership (1 Tim. 3; Titus 2; Acts 6), depending on his or her anticipated ministry (small group, staff, church planter, and other positions).
2. The prospective leader (including interns) will begin as an apprentice leader who assists a small-group leader. No one simply "walks in" and becomes a leader overnight as is common in many churches.
3. The apprentice leader will develop leadership skills working with or in the small group three weeks a month (on-the-job training) and will gain leadership knowledge attending a CKS meeting (character, knowledge, skills training session) once a month (excluding summers).
4. Leaders who foresee full-time ministry will be mentored one-on-one by someone on the pastoral staff, depending on their future ministry goals.

Time
Long-term commitment (Interns—six months to one year)

BASEBALL DIAGRAM

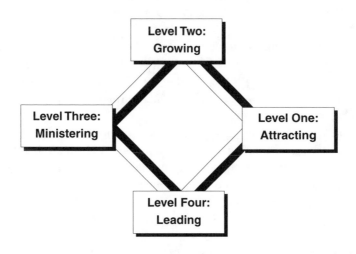

COMMENTS

The following comments provide some explanation that will help you to further understand this strategy and the rationale behind the decisions that affected it.

1. Every objective must have a corresponding strategy that implements it. An objective without a strategy is like a carpenter without a hammer or a surgeon without a scalpel.

2. It has been our experience (and that of others) that becoming a growing disciple (level 2) precedes becoming a serving or ministering disciple (level 3). The maturity that is gained in level 2 produces fruit in the form of ministry or service in level 3. This is the rationale behind having four levels.

3. The staff pastors in this system are more trainers (coaches) than doers (ministers). For example, the heavy teaching will not take place at the level 1 seeker-friendly large group meetings on Saturday or Sunday that are led by the staff. It will take place under the ministry of lay leaders in the small-group meetings at level 2. This means that the staff pastors will train the lay pastors in how to teach the deeper truths of Scripture (Eph. 4:11; 2 Tim. 2:2).

4. In a church where there are two or more staff pastors, the preaching in the seeker-friendly large group meeting will be shared by the pastors. The point person will preach perhaps 60 percent of the sermons and the support staff the other 40 percent. Consequently, should the point person leave, the church survives his loss.

5. You will need to answer the question: What purpose do the large- and small-group meetings serve? Quite frankly, it is naive to believe that the large group meeting (sermon) is sufficient in itself to disciple anyone! I know of no one who has seriously studied the disciple-making process who believes that it is. The key method in disciple making is the small group! That is how the Savior and others in the New Testament (Paul, Barnabas, and others) made disciples!

6. The measure of success in this system is not how well you know the Bible and theology nor your ability to sight read the Old and New Testaments from the original languages, and so on. While these are important, the biblical measure of your success is your disciples (Col. 1:28–29; 2 Cor. 3:1–6; Eph. 5:25–27). Where are your disciples! (If disciple making is what the church and ministry are all about, then perhaps a requirement for graduation from seminaries should not be good grades but mature disciples.)

7. The fully functioning small-group approach will replace any traditional lecture-them-to-discipleship approach for all ages. For example, children will be in their own age-group small group with a lay pastor-leader who may be an adult or possibly a mature level 4 teen leader.

8. Our programs are set up to minister to churched and unchurched, lost and saved, whether children, young people, or adults, and those who are emotionally healthy as well as those who struggle with various addictions.

9. The implementation of the various parts of this strategy is dependent on having the right people to lead them. Rather than use anyone, we will wait until we have the right person for the ministry before implementing that ministry. We will determine this based on our Divine Design Program as led by a lay or staff ministry consultant who will assist our people in discovering their ministry designs and directions and then help place them.

10. The senior or point pastor is responsible for coordinating all four levels. He will recruit, develop, and work with a gifted, qualified lay person or professional staff person to lead at each level. Preferably this person would be a lay person (especially in smaller churches and church planting; however, the problem here is turnover in our highly mobile culture). The leaders at each level are the following: (level 1) a pastor or director of programming or worship; (level 2) a pastor or director of small groups or ministries

or Christian education; (level 3) a pastor or director of involvement or administration; and (level 4) a pastor or director of leadership development. These leaders, in turn, will recruit and develop a team to minister at each level. They will be evaluated on how well they recruit their teams and produce results in each of their areas.

11. It is critical that everyone on the leadership team embrace the mission and the general strategy. That includes board members, professional and lay staff. Consequently, any discussions and disagreements will be over the details, not the general direction.

12. As God provides various people with gifts, talents, and knowledge of certain special areas, they will offer to help train our people in a class or seminar format. This would include such areas as Bible-study methods, books of the Bible, areas of theology, prayer, finances, evangelism, apologetics, and so on. The various small groups may pull together for a seminar or the instructor may visit the small group.

QUESTIONS FOR DISCUSSION AND REFLECTION

1. What do you like about the sample mission statement? Why? What do you not like about it? Why? How might it help you to write yours? What other adjectives and nouns might you use to express yours?

2. What do you like about the specific goals? Why? What do you dislike? Are they trying to say too much? Should they be expressed in terms of discipleship only? Do you agree that growing as a disciple precedes serving as a disciple? Why or why not? How many goals would you have?

3. Do you agree with the sample traits of a disciple? Do you disagree with any of the traits? If yes, which ones? Why? What traits would you include or put in their place? Is the description beneath each helpful or distracting? What might you put as some of your descriptions?

4. Do you agree with the number of levels of commitment (four)? If not, how many would you have? Would you call them *levels*, or would you use some other term? If the latter, what term would you use?

5. What is the purpose of preaching in this sample strategy? Why? What would the purpose of preaching be in your strategy? Would

you primarily depend on it to disciple your people? How good a communicator does a preacher have to be to disciple people from the pulpit?

6. Are small groups simply a fad or a necessary part of a church's strategy? How does the sample strategy use small groups? Will small groups be a part of your strategy? Why or why not? If so, what role will they play?

7. How does the sample strategy incorporate evangelism? How evangelistic will your ministry be? Will you incorporate evangelism in your strategy? If yes, how? Do you plan to target unchurched lost people or believers?

8. Will the recruitment and development of leaders be a priority of your ministry? Why or why not? How does the strategy accomplish leadership development? How might you accomplish leadership development? Will there be any one-on-one mentoring? Will you take seriously the training of interns?

9. Will lay mobilization be a priority in your ministry? Why or why not? How does the sample strategy mobilize Christians? Do you like this plan? Why or why not? Do you have a strategy for lay mobilization? What is it?

10. What is the measure of success in the sample strategy? Is it biblical? What will be the measure of success for your strategy? Why? Is it biblical?

CHAPTER TEN

Other Strategies
for Making Disciples

HERE'S MORE HELP!

The insight to recognize the gifts and abilities of others and to learn from them is a refreshing blend of humility and wisdom.

Pastor Robert Smith is both excited and relieved. He has just put the finishing touches on the strategy for Faith Chapel Church two days before the board-mandated deadline. He believes that it is a quality piece of work. If the board agrees, then he is convinced that Faith Chapel could have a strong impact on its target group in its new community. He realizes that the board meeting and future meetings with the church over their strategy will be the greatest test of his leadership since coming to Faith Chapel.

He has crafted the strategy in the context of his passion for the church. His love for Christ's church has motivated him to pour himself and all his creativity into this strategic document. While it has come from his soul, he has not crafted it in isolation. At times he has had some original thoughts and ideas; however, his creative abilities lie in taking bits and pieces of others' creative thinking and running with them. Not only has he studied his professor's sample strategy for making disciples, but he has mined some nuggets from other disciple-making churches and studied how several parachurch ministries develop their disciples. This has proven to be immensely valuable.

The purpose of this final chapter is to provide you with the strategies of several successful disciple-making churches and parachurch ministries.

As you develop a strategy for your ministry, the churches will give you some ideas of what others have done. Several parachurch organizations have specialized in making disciples and can teach the local church many helpful concepts and principles in disciple making. I would encourage you to learn from these ministries but not attempt to mimic them because they are designed to reach their unique target groups in their part of the world. It is important that your strategy reflect the unique composition and opportunities of your church.

WILLOW CREEK COMMUNITY CHURCH

Willow Creek Community Church is located in Barrington, Illinois, a suburb of Chicago. Several church planters led by Bill Hybels started Willow Creek in 1975, and it has grown to be one of the largest churches in America. What is impressive is not so much its size but that the majority of its people have come to faith and maturity as the result of the ministry of this church. Carl George observes that most large ministries are receptor churches. They continue to grow not as the result of evangelism but people transferring from other small churches. Willow Creek has defied this trend and regularly updates its ministries and seeks to do whatever it takes to accomplish God's purpose for its ministry.

Key to Willow Creek's growth and blessing is a clear, significant mission statement and strategy. The church is a new paradigm ministry that has worked hard at crafting and recrafting a strategy that implements its biblical mission.

Mission

The mission of Willow Creek Community Church is to turn irreligious people into fully devoted followers of Jesus Christ.[1] The following fourfold statement of purpose expands and explains this mission.

Exaltation: Willow Creek Community Church exists to offer the body of believers the opportunity to worship and glorify God together.

Edification: Willow Creek Community Church exists to help believers build a foundation of biblical understanding, establish a devotional life, discover their spiritual gifts, and to encourage believers to become participating members in the body of Christ.

Evangelism: Willow Creek Community Church exists to reach people who are facing a Christless eternity. Members of the body are encouraged to seek out the unchurched as the Holy Spirit has sought them out, and to look for opportunities to share Christ's love.

Social Action: Willow Creek Community Church exists to act as a conscience to the world by demonstrating the love and righteousness of God in both word and deed.[2]

Strategy

Willow Creek Community Church has developed the following seven-step strategy to accomplish the above mission statement (fig. 10.1).

Bridge building

Every believer attending Willow Creek Community Church is strongly challenged to build a relationship of integrity with their unchurched friends (Program: Use an Evangelism Ministry team that offers seminars and classes).

Sharing a verbal witness

Once a relationship of integrity has been established, believers will have an opportunity to share their testimony with unchurched Harry or Mary, the church's target group. (Program: Same as bridge building).

Providing a service for seekers

Most unchurched who hear about a believer's relationship with Christ will not immediately respond with a decision to establish a similar relationship. It is at this point that believers need a place to bring their unchurched friends so that they will continue to be challenged in a relevant creative and contemporary way to consider the claims of Christ (Program: A seeker-sensitive service on the weekends designed to supplement the believer's evangelistic efforts).

Attending the New Community service

Once someone has accepted Jesus as Savior and has been attending the weekend service for a time, he is encouraged to become involved in the midweek believer's service that provides believers with the opportunity to participate in corporate worship and to listen to expository teaching designed to mature the believer. This service is imperative for those who are committed to becoming fully devoted followers of Christ (Program: A midweek service specifically for believers focusing on worship, in-depth Bible study, and prayer).

Willow Creek's 7-Step Philosophy of Ministry

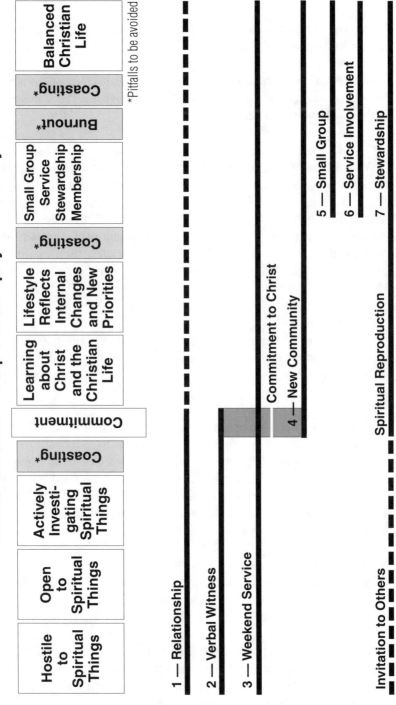

Figure 10.1

Participating in a small group

Believers who are involved in New Community are encouraged to take the next step in their Christian walk by participating in a small group that provides fellowship for the believer as well as a group for accountability, discipleship, encouragement, and support (Program: Small group ministries).

Involved in service

Believers who consider Willow Creek Community Church their home church are encouraged to discover their spiritual gift(s), develop them, and then use them in some form of Christian service within the body of Christ (Program: The Network Ministry and its seminars help believers discover their gifts and connect with ministry).

Stewardship

Believers need to be educated in the area of money management and to recognize their individual responsibility to manage their money in a God-glorifying manner. It is important that every believer recognize that stewardship is a form of discipleship and that giving is a form of worship (Program: Uses the Good Sense Ministry Team to conduct seminars on biblical foundations for money management; also has a team of trained budget counselors for family budget counseling).[3]

SADDLEBACK VALLEY COMMUNITY CHURCH

Rick Warren is the founding pastor of Saddleback Valley Community Church, a Southern Baptist ministry, located in Mission Viejo, California, south of Los Angeles. The church began in 1980 with just two families and currently has from eight thousand to ten thousand people in attendance. Rick's passion is to reach the unchurched of his community with the gospel of Christ and see them grow to maturity. Consequently, approximately 70 percent of the membership has accepted the Savior through the witness of this church. Saddleback has also sponsored fifteen daughter churches in the time that Rick has been its pastor.

Mission

The mission of Saddleback Valley Community Church is to bring people to Jesus and *membership* in his family, develop them to Christlike *maturity*, and equip them for *ministry* in the church and life *mission* in the world, in order to *magnify* God's name.[4]

The following fivefold statement of purpose serves to further clarify this mission statement. Saddleback Community Church exists to celebrate God's presence in worship (magnify), to communicate God's Word through evangelism (mission), to incorporate God's family into our fellowship (membership), to educate God's people through discipleship (maturity), and to demonstrate God's love through service (ministry).[5]

Strategy

Saddleback's strategy consists of five levels of commitment. They desire to move people from the first, which is community (unchurched lost people), to the last, which is the core (the dedicated minority of workers and leaders).

Evangelism

To have impact on the community—the pool of lost who live within driving distance of the church (uses an annual series of community-wide Bridge Events: concerts, special services, and productions).

Worship

To reach the crowd—the believers and unbelievers who attend one of the worship services every weekend (uses the weekend seeker service).

Fellowship

To move the crowd into the congregation-the church's official members (uses Class 101 and a small-group network; see fig. 10.2).

Discipleship

To move the congregation to commitment—people who are serious about their faith but aren't actively serving a church ministry (use the midweek service and the Life Development Institute: Bible studies, seminars [Class 201], workshops, independent study programs, and so on).

Ministry

To bring the committed into the core-the dedicated minority of workers and leaders (use the monthly S.A.L.T. [Saddleback Advanced Leadership Training] meeting and Class 301).[6]

Saddleback's C.L.A.S.S. Strategy

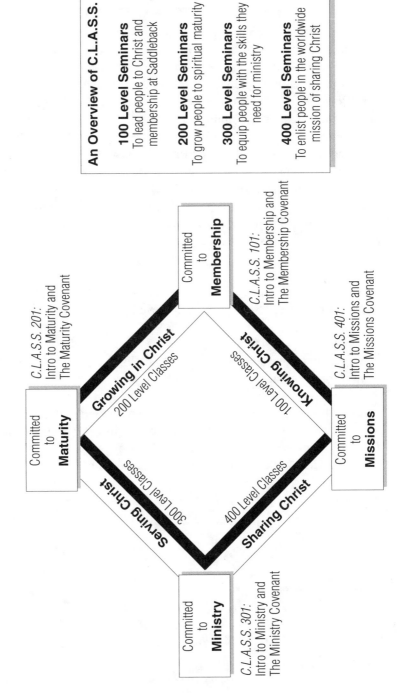

An Overview of C.L.A.S.S.

100 Level Seminars
To lead people to Christ and membership at Saddleback

200 Level Seminars
To grow people to spiritual maturity

300 Level Seminars
To equip people with the skills they need for ministry

400 Level Seminars
To enlist people in the worldwide mission of sharing Christ

Committed to **Membership**

C.L.A.S.S. 101:
Intro to Membership and The Membership Covenant

C.L.A.S.S. 201:
Intro to Maturity and The Maturity Covenant

Committed to **Maturity**

C.L.A.S.S. 401:
Intro to Missions and The Missions Covenant

Committed to **Missions**

C.L.A.S.S. 301:
Intro to Ministry and The Ministry Covenant

Committed to **Ministry**

Growing in Christ
200 Level Classes

Knowing Christ
100 Level Classes

Serving Christ
300 Level Classes

Sharing Christ
400 Level Classes

Figure 10.2

PANTEGO BIBLE CHURCH

Pantego Bible Church, a part of the Bible Church movement that flourished in the days following World War II, is located in Arlington, Texas, between Dallas and Fort Worth. Its first pastor spent twenty-five years with the church and led it to significant growth. However, in the mid to late 1970s, a crisis developed that resulted in significant decline. The worship attendance plummeted from 1,300 to 425 and contributions to the general fund went from $16,000 a week to $4,000 a week.

In February of 1990, Randy Frazee became the senior pastor and implemented a mission and strategy that has led the church out of its comfort zone. It is targeting the unchurched that make up 74 percent of the 270,000 Arlington residents. In just four years, the worship attendance has climbed from 425 to more than 1,200, and the offerings have increased at a rate of 20 to 25 percent each year.

Mission

The mission of Pantego Bible Church is to transform people, through the work of the Holy Spirit, into fully developing followers of Christ.[7]

Strategy

The strategy consists of four stages based on Acts 2:42–47 (teaching, fellowship, the breaking of bread, and prayer).[8]

Stage One: Establishing a relationship with God (a believer)
Stage Two: Putting God at the center of my life (a worshiping believer)
Stage Three: Applying God's principles to my life (a growing believer)
Stage Four: Making an impact with my life (a serving believer)

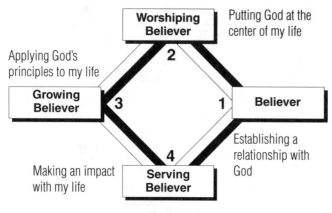

Figure 10.3

THE EVANGELICAL FREE CHURCH

The Evangelical Free Church has adopted the T-Net Program that is based on Bill Hull's book *The Disciple Making Pastor*. Bill Hull, Bob Gilliam, and others are conducting seminars around the country at which they are sharing disciple-making principles not only with Evangelical Free churches but any who are interested in reaching their world for Christ. They provide the following mission and strategy.[9]

Mission

The church's mission is to make every willing person a healthy, reproducing believer.[10]

Strategy

The strategy consists of four phases.

Phase 1:   "Come and See"
Objective: To introduce to Christ and his work
Vehicles: Sunday morning worship service, the mini-congregation (small groups), and Velcro ministries (choirs, sports teams, men's clubs, children's activities, etc.)

Phase 2:   "Come and Follow Me"
Objective: To train and establish people as mature disciples
Vehicle: Training in the Word of God, prayer, fellowship (relationships), and witnessing (outreach) in the context of a discipleship small group.

Phase 3:   "Come and Be with Me"
Objective: To select and train leadership
Vehicles: The classroom (learn six ministry skills) and on-the-job training (leading a small group, labor team, etc.)

Phase 4:   "Remain in Me"
Objective: To deploy professional leaders in professional ministries and lay leaders in local ministries
Vehicles: Professional leaders will plant churches, pastor churches, and become missionaries; lay leaders will serve as elders, deacons, etc.

EQUIPPING THE SAINTS

God has raised up various parachurch organizations like The Navigators, Campus Crusade for Christ, and Equipping the Saints to focus on areas where the church has proved weak such as evangelism and discipleship. Therefore, it would be well worth the leader's time to obtain their materials and investigate what they are doing and how they are doing it.

David Dawson was the National Director for The Navigators in the nation of Singapore when he developed Equipping the Saints (ETS). It is a parachurch ministry designed to help churches and missions agencies train lay people to make disciples. The initial challenge was to train people in the local church as effectively as they had through the parachurch or Navigators. This meant that David would have to condense what was normally anywhere from two to five years of training into a shorter time—at the most three to six weeks. Dawson developed the ETS program over a six-year involvement with a group of Singapore churches. During this time, it also underwent extensive field testing.[11]

The ETS program emphasizes Bible study and Scripture memorization. It is organized around the following ten major subject areas.[12]

1. The Layman and the Great Commission
2. Personal and Spiritual Management
3. Evangelism
4. Basic Christian Living
5. Follow-up
6. Discipleship
7. Advanced Follow-up
8. Leadership
9. Christian Character
10. Visual Survey of the Bible

Under each subject area various topics are covered to develop that subject. For example, the program breaks the topic of discipleship into the following seven layers.[13]

1. Definition of Discipleship
2. A Principle of Discipleship
3. The Focal Point of Discipleship
4. Commitment to Discipleship
5. Finding the Will of God

6. Spiritual Reproduction
7. Interpersonal Relationships

QUESTIONS FOR DISCUSSION AND REFLECTION

1. Do you find it easier to learn from other church and parachurch ministries or to come up with ideas on your own? How open are you to learning from other ministries? What are the advantages and disadvantages of the two approaches? For you, which outweighs the other and why?

2. What do you like about the mission and strategy of Willow Creek Community Church? Why? What do you dislike if anything? Why? Does their size influence how effective their activities would be for your church? Why or why not?

3. What do you like about the mission and strategy of Saddleback Valley Community Church? Why? What do you not like? Why? How might what they are doing be helpful to your ministry? How might it hurt your ministry?

4. Whereas Willow Creek and Saddleback are planted church situations, Pantego Bible Church is a revitalized ministry. What do you like about the mission and strategy of Pantego Bible Church? Why? Is their situation similar to yours in any way? What might you learn from them?

5. What do you like about the mission and strategy that Bill Hull has developed in *The Disciple Making Pastor*? How might it help your ministry? Are you familiar with the T-Net program of the Evangelical Free Church? Based on the brief introduction to T-Net in this chapter, would its training be of value to your church? Why or why not?

6. What parachurch ministries are you familiar with? What are their ministry focuses? Do you have any reservations toward them or about using their ideas and training materials? If yes, why? Which ones might prove helpful to your ministry? Why or why not?

ENDNOTES

1. "A Variety of Visions," *Leadership*, summer 1994, p. 35.
2. *Pastor's Conference Notebook*, Willow Creek Community Church, 67 East Algonquin Road, South Barrington, Illinois, October 11–15, 1989, p. 1.

3. Ibid., pp. 1–7.

4. Rick Warren, *The Purpose Driven Church* (Grand Rapids, Mich.: Zondervan Publishing House, 1995), p. 107.

5. Ibid.

6. Ibid., pp. 131–34. For a full explanation of the Saddleback Strategy, order the set of tapes form The Encouraging Word, 714-587-9534, or write to P.O. Box 6080-388, Mission Viejo, CA 92690.

7. Randy Frazee with Lyle Schaller, *The Comeback Congregation* (Nashville: Abingdon Press, 1995), p. 61.

8. Ibid., pp. 61–62.

9. For information about the T-Net program, write to the following address: EFCA, Training Network, 901 East 78th. Street, Minneapolis, MN 55420.

10. Bill Hull, *The Disciple Making Pastor* (Old Tappan, N.J.: Fleming H. Revell, 1988), pp. 216–50.

11. You may obtain information and material from the following: Equipping the Saints, 4400 Moulton Street, Suite D, Greenville, TX, 75401 (903) 455-3782, fax (903) 454-8524.

12. David L. Dawson, *Equipping the Saints Introductory Guide*, Equipping the Saints, 4400 Moulton Street, Suite D, Greenville, TX, p. 10.

13. Ibid., p. 12.

Sample Budget

GENERAL EXPENSES
Church Property

	Year	Month
Mortgage	$12,000.00	$1,000.00
Utilities	6,000.00	500.00
Grounds	5,000.00	416.66
General Maintenance	3,000.00	250.00
Equipment Maintenance	2,000.00	166.66
Custodial Service	8,000.00	665.66
Insurance	7,000.00	583.33
Total:	$43,000.00	$3,582.31

Office

	Year	Month
Secretary	$20,000.00	$1,666.66
Assistant	10,000.00	833.33
Supplies	5,000.00	416.66
Answering Service	2,400.00	200.00
Total:	$37,400.00	$3,116.65

Pastors' Benefits

	Year	Month
Life Insurance	$3,000.00	$250.00
Health Insurance	5,000.00	416.66
Retirement	8,000.00	665.66
Professional Development	4,000.00	333.33
Professional Dues	2,000.00	166.66
Total:	$22,000.00	$1,832.31

MINISTRY EXPENSES

Phase 1: Interesting in Christ

Salaries

Worship Director	$36,000.00	$3,000.00
Musicians	8,400.00	700.00
Guest Speakers	2,000.00	166.66

Program Expenses

Music	$6,000.00	$500.00
Drama	5,000.00	416.66
Printing & Mailing	5,000.00	416.66
Equipment Rental	2,000.00	166.66
Total: $64,400.00		$5,366.64

Phase 2: Growing in Christ

Salaries

Pastor of Discipleship	$36,000.00	$3,000.00

Various Ministries

Children's Ministries	5,000.00	416.66
Youth Ministries	8,000.00	665.66
Special Ministries	4,000.00	333.33
Total: $53,000.00		$4,415.65

Phase 3: Ministering in Christ

Salaries

Pastor of Involvement	$36,000.00	$3,000.00

Program Expenses

Assessment Materials	2,000.00	166.66
Total: $38,000.00		$3,166.66

Phase 4: Leading in Christ

Salaries

Pastor of Leadership	$36,000.00	$3,000.00
Church Planter	24,000.00	2,000.00
Interns (2)	24,000.00	2,000.00

Missions

The Smiths	$12,000.00	$1,000.00
The Joneses	12,000.00	1,000.00
The Martins	12,000.00	1,000.00

Program Expenses

Leadership Tools	3,000.00	250.00
Total:	$123,000.00	$10,250.00

Grand Total:	$380,800.00	$31,729.22

Strategic Planning Document

This statement lays the philosophical foundation for the establishment and continuing ministry of the _____Church of (city) , (state) . It represents our understanding of the unique role God has called us to fulfill in the world, as expressed in our mission, vision, values, and strategy as we address our community's need for Christ. We believe that by clearly identifying these things, we will be better equipped to accomplish the task God has given us (Prov. 13:16).

NEED

Our immediate community consists largely of a growing number of Baby Boomers and Baby Busters. They are highly educated and 89 percent are business and professional people. For the most part, they are unchurched (80 percent) and have no relationship with Christ.

Interviews indicate that they view the typical church as out of touch and not relevant to them or their needs (on average they attend church 6.2 times per year). Yet they are genuinely interested in spiritual truth. One survey found that 85 percent believe in the Bible, 94 percent pray regularly, 82 percent believe that Christ was God, and 75 percent believe in angels.

All predictions indicate that our community will continue to experience unprecedented growth into the twenty-first century. Demographers project that two thousand people will move into this area in the next two to three years. However, there are few churches to reach them except for a few older, mainline denominations. At the same time the Mormons and Jehovah's Witnesses have targeted them and have been relatively successful as both have built new facilities within the last year.

Therefore, there exists a strong need for a culturally relevant church with a passionate desire to target and reach for the Savior these unchurched Boomers and Busters who are most interested at the present in spiritual truth.

VALUES

A Commitment to Relevant Bible Teaching

We believe that the Bible is God's inspired, trustworthy rule of faith and practice for all Christians (2 Tim. 3:16). It is both timeless and timely, relevant to all people at all times. Therefore, we are committed to equipping disciples through the teaching of Scripture to follow Christ in all areas of life.

A Commitment to Lay Ministry

We believe that the primary responsibility of the pastoral staff is to equip our people for ministry (Eph. 4:11–12). Therefore, the pastoral staff will spend much of its time in equipping our multi-gifted people to make disciples in their small group ministries.

A Commitment to Authentic Life Change

We believe that God wants all of his people to experience genuine, biblical life change which involves godliness and true holiness (1 Pet. 1:15–16). Therefore, we are committed to small group ministries as the best vehicle to make this happen.

A Commitment to Team Ministry

We believe that New Testament ministry is team ministry (Mark 6:7). Therefore, wherever and whenever possible, we will conduct our staff and lay ministries in a team context, including strong family ministries.

A Commitment to Creativity and Relevance

In today's rapidly changing world, we believe that our ministry methods are flexible while our biblical principles are fixed (1 Cor. 9:19–23). Therefore, while maintaining our principles, we will regularly evaluate and change our forms of ministry so as to remain relevant to our times (1 Chron. 12:32).

A Commitment to Excellence

We believe that our God is a God of excellence who deserves the very best we have to offer (1 Cor. 3:13). Therefore, in all our ministries and activities, we will seek to maintain the highest standards of excellence to the glory of God.

A Commitment to Growth

Although numerical growth is not a sufficient goal in itself, we believe that God wants us to reach as many people as possible with the gospel (Matt. 28:19–20). Therefore, we will pursue methods that will facilitate numerical growth without compromising our integrity or commitment to biblical truth.

MISSION

Our comprehensive mission is to do whatever it takes to see lost people become fully devoted disciples of Jesus Christ (Matt. 28:19–20).

VISION

Our vision is to honor our Lord and Savior, Jesus Christ, by carrying out his command to make disciples of all nations (Matthew 28:19–20). Specifically, we believe God has called us to focus on reaching those in this city and the surrounding areas who do not regularly attend any church.

In order to accomplish this, our church will be an equipping center where every Christian can be developed to his or her full potential for ministry. This development will come through: creative, inspiring worship; teaching that is biblical and relevant to life; vital, supportive fellowship; and opportunities for outreach into the community in service and evangelism.

As a result, our community will be different in ten to fifteen years, with the Christian influence being increasingly felt in homes, businesses, education, and politics. We further intend to multiply our worldwide ministry by planting churches, by preparing our people for leadership roles in vocational ministries and parachurch groups, by sending out missionaries, and by becoming a resource center and model for Texas and the nation.

STRATEGY

The specific goals (to realize our mission):

#1. To lead people to Christ and active involvement in our church (to interest in *becoming* a disciple)

#2. To grow people to spiritual maturity (to become a *growing* disciple)

#3. To equip for and involve people in ministry both within and outside the body of believers (to grow into a *serving* disciple)

#4. To enlist disciples for leadership locally and in the world (to serve in discipling others)

What does a fully devoted disciple look like? The biblical, measurable behavioral traits of an authentic disciple are the following:

Trait #1: A basic, growing knowledge of the Bible and applies it to his or her life (John 8:31–32)

Trait #2: A regular devotional time (prayer, worship, etc.) with God and the family (John 15:7–8)

Trait #3: A daily recommitment (putting Christ first) of one's life to Christ (Luke 9:23–25; 14:25–35)

Trait #4: Regular attendance at church and membership in a small group (Heb. 10:25; John 13:34–35;15:7–17; Acts 2:46; 5:42; 8:3; 20:20)

Trait #5: Understands his or her gifts and is involved in a ministry (1 Tim. 4:14; 2 Tim. 1:6; Eph. 4:11–13)

Trait #6: Building relationships and sharing the faith ("fishers of men") with lost people at home and abroad (Matt. 9:36–38)

Trait #7: A generous, joyful giver (2 Cor. 8).

Note: These traits are found below in parenthesis next to the objective(s) that accomplish(es) them. When a person reaches level 3, he or she is realizing the mission. While level 4 isn't necessary for one to be a fully devoted disciple, every church must develop leaders who are disciple makers.

Level 1: Interesting in Christ
Goal

- To lead people to Christ and active involvement in the church (to interest in *becoming* a disciple) (Luke 15:1–10; 19:1–10; Col. 4:2–6; 2 Tim. 4:4; 1 Cor. 14:22–25)

To call unchurched lost and saved people (young people as well as adults) out of the stands (world) and onto the playing field (serious, authentic Christianity)

Action Steps

1. A seeker-friendly large group meeting (to interest lost and saved young people and adults in becoming disciples)
   A. Sermon—mostly topical that teaches biblical truth about life's issues that matter and that shows its relevancy to everyday life

B. Drama—short, relevant accounts that set up or introduce the sermon topic and/or make application to life

C. Worship—contemporary, celebrative music led by a praise band

D. Prayer—a time of public prayer for world, nation, and community

E. Evangelism—a regular presentation of the gospel through sermons, drama, and other means

2. A small group to lead people to Christ and/or orient them to the church (its expectations, beliefs, programs, etc.). It loves and cares for them as well. These groups are in the early stages of initiating the disciple-making process. They are explaining what the church is all about and inviting those in the group to move on with Christ. Those who remain will go on with this group to phase 2 (Trait #4)

A. Basic small groups for regular people

These are communities that minister to all ages from children's groups to older adult groups. (The small group approach will replace the traditional Sunday school for our children and young people.) The ordinances (Lord's Supper and baptism) will take place in this context.

B. Special small groups for special people

Twelve-step Groups, Addiction Groups, Abuse Groups, Women's and Men's Groups, Premarriage Groups, Divorce Recovery Groups, etc.

3. Other events (to minister to people and hold them in the church) such as vacation Bible school, aerobics, choir, Pioneer Boys and Girls Clubs, Awana, sports events, etc.

Time

How long should a person be at level 1? Six months? One to two years? The average seeker takes from six to twelve months to accept Christ.

> Note: Both the large- and small-group leaders constantly invite these people to become fully devoted disciples, that is, to move to level 2.

Level 2: Growing in Christ

Goal

- To grow people to spiritual maturity (to become a growing disciple) (Col. 1:28; Eph. 4:12–13; 1 Tim. 4:7–8; Heb. 6:1–3)

Action Steps

Discipleship Small Groups (fully functioning communities)

Lay pastor-leaders will equip the people in their small groups in each of the following key areas that are essential to becoming a disciple:

1. Scripture—to gain a knowledge of the Bible, theology, and how to study the Bible on one's own (Trait #1)
2. Prayer—to learn about and practice private and public prayer (Trait #2)
3. Worship—to learn about and practice private and public worship (Trait #2)
4. Evangelism—to discover one's evangelism style and begin to share the Gospel with the lost in his/her relational group, community, and the world (missions) (Trait #6)
5. Giving—to learn about biblical giving and practice it (Trait #7)
6. Commitment—to learn the importance of and commit to attending the meetings of the church. More important to commit one's life to the Lord daily (Traits # 3 and #4)

Time

One to two years?

Level 3: Ministering in Christ
Goal

- To equip people for and involve them in ministry (to become a serving disciple) (Eph. 4:11–12; 1 Cor. 12:12–31; Rom. 12:1–8; 1 Tim. 4:14)

This lay mobilization primarily involves helping people to discover their gifts, direction, and ministry placement so that they can become Christ's servants (servanthood). Their ministry may take place within the four walls of the church or outside in the local community—inner-city mission, church planting, etc.

Action Steps

1. The person will continue in his or her discipleship small group.
2. A professional or lay minister of involvement will visit the group and take them through the Lay Mobilization process and direct them to an existing ministry fit or start a new ministry (Trait #5).

Time

One to three months?

Level 4: Leading in Christ
Goal

- To enlist disciples as lay and professional leaders of ministries at home and abroad (to become disciple makers) (1 Tim. 3:1–13; Acts 6:1–7; 2 Tim. 2:2; Titus 1:1–9)

These leaders will become small-group leaders, deacons, elders, church staff, church planters, and missionaries of the church (Trait #6). It is a process and no one becomes a leader overnight! (Interns from seminaries, Bible colleges, and Christian schools will do their internships in phase 4.)

> Note: Not everyone who is a disciple is expected to move to level 4. This is for a select group who are key to the ministry. The staff and small group leaders in particular look for these gifted leaders (including mature teenagers) and individually invite and encourage them to consider moving on to level 4. The staff and others will pour much of their time and lives into these potential leaders.

Strategy

1. The prospective leader must meet certain requirements for leadership (e.g., 1 Tim. 3; Titus 2, etc.), depending on his/her anticipated ministry (small group, staff, church planter, etc.).
2. The prospective leader (including interns) will begin as an apprentice leader, assisting a small-group leader. No one simply walks in and becomes a leader overnight.
3. The apprentice leader will develop leadership skills working with/in the small group three weeks a month (OJT) and will gain leadership knowledge attending a CKS (character, knowledge, skills training session) meeting once a month (excluding summers).
4. Leaders who foresee full-time ministry will be mentored one on one by someone on the pastoral staff, depending on their future ministry goals.

Time

Long-term commitment (Interns—six months to one year)

BASEBALL DIAGRAM

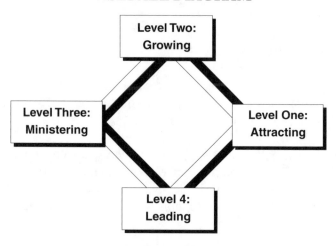

COMMENTS

1. Every objective must have a corresponding action step that implements it. An objective without a strategy is like a carpenter without a hammer or a surgeon without a scalpel.

2. It has been our experience (and that of others) that becoming a growing disciple (level 2) precedes becoming a serving/ministering disciple (level 3). The maturity that is gained on level 2 produces fruit in the form of ministry or service on level 3. This is the rationale behind having four phases.

3. The staff pastors in this system are more trainers (coaches) than doers (ministers). For example, the heavy teaching will not take place at level 1 seeker-friendly large group meetings on Saturday or Sunday that are led by the staff. It will take place under the ministry of lay leaders in the small group meetings at level 2. This means that the staff pastors will train the lay pastors in how to teach the deeper truths of Scripture (Eph. 4:11; 2 Tim. 2:2).

4. In a church where there are two or more staff pastors, the preaching in the seeker-friendly large group meeting will be shared by the pastors. The point person will preach 60 percent of the sermons and the support staff the other 40 percent. Consequently, should the point person leave, the church survives his loss.

5. You will need to answer the question: What purpose does the large group and the small group meetings serve? Quite frankly, it is naive to believe that the large group meeting (sermon) is sufficient in itself to disciple anyone! I know of no one who has seriously

studied the disciple-making process who believes that it is. The key method in disciple making is the small group! That is how the Savior and others in the New Testament (Paul, Barnabas, etc.) made disciples!

6. The measure of success in this system is not how well you know the Bible and theology nor your ability to sight-read the Old and New Testaments from the original languages, etc. While these are important, the biblical measure of your success is your disciples (Col. 1:28–29; 2 Cor. 3:1–6; Eph. 5:25–27). Where are your disciples! (If disciple making is what the church and ministry are all about, then perhaps a requirement for graduation from seminaries should not be good grades but mature disciples.)

7. The fully functioning small-group approach will replace any traditional lecture-them-to-discipleship approach for all ages. For example, children will be in their own age-group small group with a lay pastor-leader who may be an adult or possibly a mature phase 4 teen leader.

8. Our programs are set up to minister to churched and unchurched, lost and saved, whether children, young people, or adults, and those who are emotionally healthy as well as those who struggle with various addictions.

9. The implementation of the various parts of this strategy is dependent on having the right people to lead them. Rather than use anyone, we will wait until we have the right person for the ministry before implementing that ministry. We will determine this based on our Divine Design Program as led by a lay or staff ministry consultant who will assist our people in discovering their ministry designs and directions and then help place them.

10. The senior or point pastor is responsible for coordinating all four levels. He will recruit, develop, and work with a gifted, qualified lay person or professional staff person to lead at each level. Preferably this person would be a lay person (especially in smaller churches and church planting; however, the problem here is turnover in our highly mobile culture). The leaders at each level are the following: (level 1) a pastor/director of programming or worship; (level 2) a pastor/director of small groups or ministries or Christian education; (level 3) a pastor/director of involvement or administration; and (level 4) a pastor/director of leadership development. These leaders, in turn, will recruit and develop a team to minister at each level.

Strategy For Discipleship I

(FOUR-LEVEL MODEL)

MISSION

"The mission of the church is to make fully devoted disciples" (Matt. 28:19–20; Mark 16:15; Luke 24:47; Acts 1:8).

The specific steps (to realize the mission):

#1. To lead people to Christ and active involvement in our church (to interest in *becoming* a disciple)

#2. To grow people to spiritual maturity (to become a *growing* disciple)

#3. To equip for and involve a person in ministry both within and outside the body of believers (to become a *serving* disciple)

#4. To enlist disciples for leadership locally and in the world (to serve in discipling others)

The measurable, biblical behavioral traits of an authentic disciple.

Trait #1: A basic, growing knowledge of the Bible and applies it to his or her life (John 8:31–32)

We will help you to understand how the Bible is organized into the Old and New Testament and the general contents of each. You will know where to go for wisdom (Proverbs, James), worship (Psalms), etc. You will also gain a knowledge of basic Bible study skills. We will coach you to regularly ask the question: So what? What difference will this biblical truth make in my life, marriage, work, etc. today, tomorrow, next year?

Trait #2: A regular devotional time (prayer, worship, etc.) with God and the family (John 15:7–8)

We will coach and encourage you to spend regular devotional time individually and with your family. We will instruct you in the various ways to accomplish this, and you will see it modeled in the lives and families of others.

Trait #3: A daily recommitment (putting Christ first) of one's life to Christ (Luke 9:23–25; 14:25–35)

We will encourage and exhort you to make a total commitment of your life to Christ as one of your most important life decisions. In addition, we will supply encouragement and accountability so that you might follow this up with a weekly or better a daily recommitment of yourself and all that you own to Him (Rom. 6–8; 12:1–2).

Trait #4: Regular attendance at church and membership in a small group (Heb. 10:25; John 13:34–35; 15:7–17; Acts 2:46; 5:42; 8:3; 20:20)

We have designed our large group meetings to address the relevant issues of our daily lives from the Scriptures as we worship God together. We are not a church *with* small groups but a church *of* small groups. Therefore, we also request that you become a vital part of one of our vibrant small groups where much of our discipleship takes place.

Trait #5: Understands his or her gifts and is involved in a ministry (1 Tim. 4:14; 2 Tim. 1:6; Eph. 4:11–13)

God has wonderfully designed all of us in a unique way to serve him. He has called and gifted us to be his servants whether within or outside the four walls of the church. It is our goal to help you discover who you are, like who you are, and be who you are while serving the Savior.

Trait #6: Building relationships and sharing the faith ("a fisher of people") with lost people at home and abroad (Matt. 9:36–38)

Because lost people matter to God, they matter to us (Luke 15; 19:1–10). We desire to do whatever it takes to help you reach the toughest mission field of your life—your neighbors, family, and workmates.

Trait #7: A generous, joyful giver (2 Cor. 8)

All that we possess is a gracious gift from God that ultimately belongs to him. Therefore, we will provide you with instruction on biblical giving and encourage you to invest in God's work throughout this ministry.

Note: These traits are found below in parentheses next to the objective(s) that accomplish(es) them.

STRATEGY

The following strategy is how we move people from prebirth to maturity. It consists of four levels that represent increasing levels of commitment.

Note: When a person reaches level 3, he or she is realizing the mission. While level 4 isn't necessary for one to be a fully devoted disciple, every church must develop leaders who are disciple-makers.

Level 1: Interesting in Christ
Goal

- To lead people to Christ and membership in the church (to interest in *becoming* a disciple) (Luke 15:1–10; 19:1–10; Col. 4:2–6; 2 Tim. 4:4; 1 Cor. 14:22–25)

To call unchurched lost and saved people (young people as well as adults) out of the stands (world) and onto the playing field (serious, authentic Christianity

Action Steps

1. A seeker-friendly large group meeting (to interest lost and saved young people and adults in becoming disciples). This is a "front door" event.
    - A. Sermon—mostly topical that teaches biblical truth and shows its relevancy to everyday life
    - B. Drama—short, relevant accounts that set up or introduce sermon topic and/or make application to life
    - C. Worship—contemporary, celebrative music led by a praise band
    - D. Prayer—a time of public prayer for world, nation, and community
    - E. Evangelism—a regular presentation of the gospel through sermons, drama, etc.
2. A small group to lead people to Christ and/or orient them to the

church (its expectations, beliefs, programs, etc.). It loves and cares for them as well. These groups are in the early stages of initiating the disciple-making process. They are explaining what the church is all about and inviting those in the group to move on with Christ. Those who stick go on with this group to level 2 (Trait #4).

A. Basic small groups for regular people

These are communities that minister to all ages from children's groups to older adult groups. (The small-group approach will replace the traditional Sunday school for our children and young people.) The ordinances will take place in this context (Lord's Supper and baptism).

B. Special small groups for special people

Twelve-step Groups, Addiction Groups, Abuse Groups, Women's and Men's Groups, Premarriage Groups, Divorce Recovery Groups, etc.

3. Other events (to minister to people and hold them in the church). vacation Bible school, aerobics, choir, Pioneer Boys and Girls Clubs, Awana, Sports events, etc.

Time

How long should a person be in phase 1? One to two years?

Note: Both the large- and small-group leaders constantly invite these people to become fully devoted disciples, that is, to move to phase 2.

Level 2: Growing in Christ
Goal

• To grow people to spiritual maturity (to become a growing disciple) (Col. 1:28; Eph. 4:12–13; 1 Tim. 4:7–8; Heb. 6:1–3)

Action Steps

Discipleship Small Groups (fully functioning communities)

Lay pastor-leaders will equip the people in their small groups in each of the following key areas that are essential to becoming a disciple:

1. Scripture—to gain a knowledge of the Bible, theology, and how to study the Bible on one's own (Trait #1)
2. Prayer—to learn about and practice private and public prayer (Trait #2)
3. Worship—to learn how to and practice private and public worship (Trait #2)

4. Evangelism—to discover one's evangelism style and begin to share gospel with the lost in his/her relational group, community, and the world through missions (Trait #6)
5. Giving—to learn about biblical giving and practice it (Trait #7)
6. Commitment—to learn the importance of and commit to attending the meetings of the church. More importantly, to commit one's life to the Lord daily (Traits # 3 and #4)

Time
One to two years?

Level 3: Ministering in Christ
Goal
- To equip people for and involve them in ministry (to become a serving disciple) (Eph. 4:11–12; 1 Cor. 12:12–31; Rom. 12:1–8; 1 Tim. 4:14)

This level primarily involves helping people to discover their gifts, direction, and ministry placement so that they can become Christ's servants (servanthood). Their ministry may take place within the church building or in the local community with an inner-city mission, church planting team, youth ministry team, etc.

Action Steps
1. The person will continue in his/her discipleship small group.
2. A professional or lay minister of involvement will visit the group and take them through a lay mobilization process and direct them to an existing ministry or start a new ministry (Trait #5).

Time
One to three months?

Level 4: Leading in Christ
Goal
- To enlist disciples as lay and professional leaders of ministries at home and abroad (to become disciple makers) (1 Tim. 3:1–13; Titus 1:1–9; Acts 6:1–7; 2 Tim. 2:2)

These leaders will become small group leaders, deacons, elders, church staff, church planters, and missionaries of the church (Trait #6). It is a process, and no one becomes a leader overnight! Interns from seminaries, Bible colleges, and Christian schools will do their internships at this level.

Note: Not everyone who is a disciple is expected to move to level 4. This is for those who show strong potential for ministry leadership. The staff and small group leaders in particular look for these gifted leaders (including mature teenagers) and individually invite and encourage them to consider moving on to level 4. The staff and group leaders will pour much of their time and lives into these potential leaders.

Strategy

1. The prospective leader must meet certain requirements for leadership (e.g., 1 Tim. 3; Titus 2, etc.), depending on his/her anticipated ministry (small group, staff, church planter, etc.).
2. The prospective leader (including interns) will begin as an apprentice leader, assisting a small-group leader. No one should be allowed to simply "walk in" and become a leader overnight.
3. The apprentice leader will develop leadership skills working with/in the small group three weeks a month (on the job training) and will gain leadership knowledge attending a CKS (character, knowledge, skills training session) meeting once a month (excluding summers).
4. Leaders-in-training who foresee full-time ministry will be mentored one on one by someone on the pastoral staff, depending on their future ministry goals.

Time

Long-term commitment (Interns—six months to one year)

BASEBALL DIAGRAM

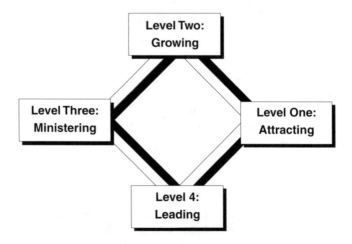

Level Two: Growing

Level Three: Ministering

Level One: Attracting

Level 4: Leading

COMMENTS

1. Every objective must have a corresponding strategy that implements it. An objective without a strategy is like a carpenter without a hammer or a surgeon without a scalpel.

2. It has been our experience (and that of others) that becoming a growing disciple (level 2) precedes becoming a serving/ministering disciple (level 3). The maturity that is gained in level 2 produces fruit in the form of ministry or service at level 3. This is the rationale behind having four levels.

3. The staff pastors in this system are more trainers (coaches) than doers (ministers). For example, the heavy teaching will not take place in the level 1 seeker-friendly large group meetings on Saturday or Sunday that are led by the staff. It will take place under the ministry of lay leaders in the small group meetings at level 2. This means that the staff pastors will train the lay pastors in how to teach the deeper truths of Scripture (Eph. 4:11, 2 Tim. 2:2).

4. In a church where there are two or more staff pastors, the preaching in the seeker-friendly large group meeting will be shared by the pastors. The point person will preach 60 percent of the sermons and the support staff the other 40 percent. Consequently, should the point person leave, the church survives his loss.

5. You will need to answer the question: What purpose do the large group and the small group meetings serve? Quite frankly, it is naive to believe that the large group meeting (sermon) is sufficient in itself to disciple anyone! I know of no one who has seriously studied the disciple-making process who believes that it is. The key method in disciple making is the small group. That is how the Savior and others in the New Testament (Paul, Barnabas, etc.) made disciples!

6. The measure of success in this approach is not how well you know the Bible and theology nor your ability to sight-read the Old and New Testaments from the original languages. While these are important, the biblical measure of your success is your disciples (Col. 1:28–29; 2 Cor. 3:1–6; Eph. 5:25–27). Where are your disciples? (If disciple making is what the church and ministry are all about, then perhaps a requirement for graduation from seminaries should not be good grades but mature disciples.)

7. The fully functioning small-group approach will replace any traditional lecture-them-to-discipleship approach for all ages. For example, children will be in their own age-group small group with

a lay pastor-leader who may be an adult or possibly a mature level 4 teen leader.

8. Programs should be set up to minister to churched and unchurched, lost and saved, whether children, young people, or adults, and those who are emotionally healthy as well as those who struggle with various addictions.

9. The implementation of the various parts of this strategy is dependent on having the right people to lead them. Rather than use anyone, we will wait until we have the right person for the ministry before implementing that ministry. We will determine this based on our Divine Design Program as led by a lay or staff ministry consultant who will assist our people in discovering their ministry designs and directions and then help place them.

10. The senior or point pastor is responsible for coordinating all four levels. He will recruit, develop, and work with a gifted, qualified lay person or professional staff person to lead at each level. Preferably this person would be a lay person (especially in smaller churches and church planting; however, the problem here is turnover in our highly mobile culture). The leaders at each level are the following: (level 1) a pastor or director of programming or worship; (level 2) a pastor or director of small groups or ministries or Christian education; (level 3) a pastor or director of involvement or administration; and (level 4) a pastor or director of leadership development. These leaders, in turn, will recruit and develop a team to minister at each level. They will be evaluated on how well they recruit their teams, and produce results in each of their areas.

11. It is critical that everyone on the leadership team embrace the mission and the general strategy. This includes board members as well as professional and lay staff. Consequently, any discussions and disagreements will be over the details, not the general direction.

12. As God provides various people with gifts, talents, and knowledge of certain special areas, they will offer to help train people in a class or seminar format. This would include such areas as Bible study methods, books of the Bible, areas of theology, prayer, finances, evangelism, apologetics, etc. The various small groups may pull together for a seminar or the instructor may visit the small group.

Strategy for Discipleship II

(FIVE-LEVEL MODEL)

MISSION

The mission of the church is to make fully devoted disciples (Matt. 28:19–20; Mark 16:15; Luke 24:47; Acts 1:8). This is a discipleship-driven mission.

The specific steps (to realize the mission):

#1. To make contact with unchurched lost people in order to expose them to the Savior and authentic Christianity (to interest in *becoming* a disciple)

#2. To lead people to Christ and active involvement in our church (to become a *growing* disciple)

#3. To grow people to spiritual maturity (to grow into a *serving* disciple)

#4. To equip for and involve a person in ministry both within and outside the body of believers (to become a *serving* disciple)

#5. To enlist disciples for leadership locally and in the world (to serve in discipling others)

The measurable, biblical behavioral traits of an authentic disciple:

Trait #1: A basic, growing knowledge of the Bible and applies it to his/her life (John 8:31–32)

The disciple will understand how the Bible is organized into the Old and New Testament and the general contents of each. He/she will know where to go for wisdom (Proverbs, James), worship (Psalms), etc. He/she will have a knowledge of basic Bible study skills. The disciple will be coached to regularly ask the question: So what? What difference will this biblical truth make in my thinking, habits, family relationships, and work for this week, this month, or this year? The basic goal is to spend some time every day reading and reflecting on the Scriptures.

Trait #2: A regular devotional time (prayer, worship, etc.) with God and the family (John 15:7–8)

The disciple will learn the importance of a regular devotional time individually and with his/her family. He/she will receive instruction in various ways to accomplish this and will see it modeled in the lives and families of others. Then he/she will set up a daily devotional time.

Trait #3: A daily recommitment (putting Christ first) of one's life to Christ (Luke 9:23–25; 14:25–35)

The disciple will learn that a once-for-all commitment of one's life to Christ is important. However, it must be followed up with a regular, weekly or, better, a daily recommitment of one's time, treasures, and talents if it is to become a reality (Rom. 12:1–2). The disciple will recommit his/her life to Christ every day during the daily devotional time.

Trait #4: Regular attendance at church and membership in a small group (Heb. 10:25; John 13:34–35; 15:7–17; Acts 2:46; 5:42; 8:3; 20:20)

As much as possible, the disciple will attempt to be present at the weekly services of the church. With the help of the pastor of discipleship, the disciple will join and faithfully be a part of a small group that focuses on where the person is on his or her spiritual journey.

Trait #5: Understands his/her gifts and is involved in a ministry (1 Tim. 4:14; 2 Tim. 1:6; Eph. 4:11–13)

The disciple will discover his/her gifts, direction, and development for ministry. This will take place in the context of his/her small group when it corporately participates in the divine design seminar. Approximately six months after the seminar, the disciple will be involved in a ministry within or outside the church.

Trait #6: Building relationships and sharing the faith ("a fisher of men") with lost people at home and abroad (Matt. 9:36–38)

The disciple looks for opportunities to evangelize according to his/her evangelism style as he/she comes into contact with people such as workmates, family members, neighbors, schoolmates, etc. The small group will corporately participate in an evangelism seminar, and much evangelism will take place in the context of the small group as it conducts various community projects. The goal is to touch one person per month.

Trait #7: A generous, joyful giver (2 Cor. 8)

The disciple will become a regular, generous joyful giver of his/her finances back to the Lord. While the Scriptures encourage grace giving as opposed to setting a certain figure or percent, an excellent gift is a tithe (approximately 10 percent).

> Note: These traits are found below in parentheses next to the objective(s) that accomplish(es) them.

STRATEGY

The following strategy is how we move people from spiritual prebirth to Christian maturity. It consists of five levels that represent increasing levels of commitment.

> Note: When a person reaches level 4, he or she is realizing the mission. While level 5 isn't necessary for one to be a fully devoted disciple, every church must develop leaders who are disciple makers.

Level 1: Interesting in Christ
Goal
- To make contact with unchurched lost and unchurched saved to expose them to Christ and authentic Christianity (to interest in *becoming* a disciple) (Luke 15:1–10; 19:1–10; Col. 4:2–6; 2 Tim. 4:4; 1 Cor. 14:22–25)

Strategy
1. A seeker-friendly large group meeting to interest lost and saved young people and adults in becoming disciples (Trait #6)
   This is a "front door" event for those who will attend a large group meeting and/or want anonymity.

A. Sermon—mostly topical that teaches biblical truth and shows its relevancy to everyday life
B. Drama—short, relevant accounts that set up or introduce sermon topic and/or make application to life
C. Worship—contemporary, celebrative music led by a praise band
D. Prayer—a time of public prayer for world, nation, and community
E. Evangelism—a regular presentation of the gospel through sermons, drama, etc.

2. Individual activities:
The church will regularly encourage its believers to build redemptive relationships with their lost friends (workmates, neighbors, classmates, and family) according to each believer's evangelism style. The church provides the seeker-friendly large group meeting (a "front door" event) and the "side door" events below to help them in their efforts to see their lost friends accept Christ (Trait #6).

3. "Side door" events:
These are church-initiated events for people who will not attend a "front door" large group meeting (hence "side door" events). Many unchurched feel that "church" is not for them, but they are attracted to events that specifically target them (Trait #6).
A. Evangelistic home Bible studies, small group gatherings where you discuss issues that concern believers and present the gospel, etc.
B. Special short-term small groups that function as support groups (engaged couples, single parents, divorced, blended families, grieving, mid-life crisis, etc.) and recovery groups (alcoholism, codependency, compulsions, addictions, abuse, depression, etc.).
C. Seminars that address people's needs, values, hopes, dreams, and aspirations. The church will offer seminars on such topics as parenting skills, how to handle anger, how to deal with worry, financial planning, etc.
D. Special sponsored events such as a 10K run, health fairs, neighborhood crime prevention meetings, etc.
E. Other methods such as mailers, surveys, a welcome wagon, a community prayer ministry, a community service project (Gal. 6:10), advertising in the newspaper (other than the church section), etc.

Time

Six to twelve months.

Level 2: Believing in Christ

Goal

- To lead people to Christ and membership in the church (to become an assimilated disciple) (John 3:16; 15:1–8; Acts 16:31; Heb. 6:1–12; 10:19–39)
- To call unchurched lost and saved people (young people as well as adults) out of the stands (world) and onto the playing field (serious, authentic Christianity)

Strategy

1. A seeker-friendly large group meeting that shows the relevancy of God's truth to everyday life and exposes people to authentic worship. The same large group service as at level 1 will serve this goal as well. Consequently, the sermon, worship, drama, etc. will be the same.
2. A small group to lead people to Christ and/or orient them to the church (its expectations, beliefs, programs, etc.). It loves and cares for them as well. These groups are in the early stages of initiating the disciple-making process. They are explaining what the church is all about and inviting those in the group to move on with Christ. Those who stick with this group go on to level 3 (Trait #4).
    A. Basic small groups for regular people.
       These are communities that minister to all ages from children's groups to older-adult groups. (The small-group approach will replace the traditional Sunday school for our children and young people.) The ordinances (Lord's Supper and baptism) will take place in this context.
    B. Special small groups for special people:
       Twelve-step groups, addiction groups, victims of abuse groups, women's and men's groups, premarriage groups, divorce recovery groups, etc.
3. Other events (to minister to people and hold them in the church): vacation Bible school, aerobics, choir, boys' and girls' clubs, sports events, etc.

Time

Maximum of one year.

Note: Both the large and small-group leaders constantly invite these people to become fully devoted disciples, that is, to move to level 2.

Level 3: Growing in Christ
Goal
- To grow people to spiritual maturity (to become a growing disciple) (Col. 1:28; Eph. 4:12–13; 1 Tim. 4:7–8; Heb. 6:1–3)

Strategy

Discipleship Small Groups (fully functioning communities).

Lay pastor-leaders will equip the people in their small groups in each of the following key areas that are essential to becoming a disciple:

1. Scripture—to gain a knowledge of the Bible, theology, and how to study the Bible on one's own (Trait #1)
2. Prayer—to learn about and practice private and public prayer (Trait #2)
3. Worship—to learn about and practice private and public worship (Trait #2)
4. Evangelism—to discover one's evangelism style and begin to share the gospel with the lost in his/her relational group, community, and the world through missions (Trait #6)
5. Giving—to learn about biblical giving and practice it (Trait #7)
6. Commitment—to learn the importance of and commit to attending the meetings of the church. More important to commit one's life to the Lord daily (Traits # 3 and #4)

Time

Two years?

Level 4: Ministering in Christ
Goal
- To equip people for and involve them in ministry (to become a serving disciple) (Eph. 4:11–12; 1 Cor. 12:12–31; Rom. 12:1–8; 1 Tim. 4:14)

This lay mobilization primarily involves helping people to discover their gifts, direction, and ministry placement so that they can become Christ's servants (servanthood). Their ministry may take place within the church building or in the local community with an inner-city mission, church planting team, youth ministry team, etc.

Strategy

1. The person will continue in his/her discipleship small group.
2. A professional or lay minister of involvement will visit the group and take them through the Lay Mobilization process and direct them to an existing ministry fit or start a new ministry (Trait #5).

Time

One to three months?

Level 5: Leading in Christ

Goal

- To enlist disciples as lay and professional leaders of ministries at home and abroad (to become disciple makers) (1 Tim. 3:1–13; Titus 1:1–9; Acts 6:1–7; 2 Tim. 2:2)

These leaders will become small-group leaders, deacons, elders, church staff, church planters, and missionaries of the church (Trait #6). It is a process and no one becomes a leader overnight! Interns from seminaries, Bible colleges, and Christian schools will do their internships at level 5.

> Note: Not everyone who is a disciple is expected to move to level 5. This is for those who show strong potential for ministry leadership. The staff and small group leaders in particular look for these gifted leaders (including mature teenagers) and individually invite and encourage them to consider moving on to level 5. The staff and others will pour much of their time and lives into these potential leaders.

Strategy

1. The prospective leader must meet certain requirements for leadership (e.g., 1 Tim. 3; Titus 2, etc.), depending on his or her anticipated ministry (small group, staff, church planter, etc.).
2. The prospective leader (including interns) will begin as an apprentice leader, assisting a small-group leader. No one simply "walks in" and becomes a leader overnight.
3. The apprentice leader will develop leadership skills working with/ in the small group three weeks a month (OJT) and will gain leadership knowledge attending a CKS (character, knowledge, skills training session) meeting once a month (excluding summers).

4. Leaders who foresee full-time ministry will be mentored one on one by someone on the pastoral staff, depending on their future ministry goals.

Time

Long-term commitment (Interns—six months to one year)

Diagram and Comments

(See p. 192)

Readiness for Change Inventory

Directions: Each item below is a key element that will help you to evaluate your church's readiness for growth. Strive for objectivity— involve others (including outsiders) in the evaluation process. Circle the number that most accurately rates your church.

1. Leadership.
- The pastor and the church board (official leadership) are eager to see the church grow and are directly responsible for it. If any influential persons (unofficial leadership such as the church patriarch, a wealthy member, etc.) are for growth, score 5.
- If the official and unofficial leadership is only moderately in favor of growth, score 3.
- If only the secondary level of leadership (other staff, Sunday school teachers, etc.) wants to see growth occur while unofficial leadership opposes it, growth is less likely to occur—score 1.

5   3   1

2. Vision.
- The pastor and the board have a single, clear vision of a significant future that looks different from the present. The pastor is able to mobilize most relevant parties (other staff, boards, and the congregation) for action—score 5.
- If the pastor but not the board envisions a different direction for the church, score 3.
- If the pastor and board have not thought about a vision, and/or they do not believe that it is important, score 1.

5   3   1

3. Values.

- The church's philosophy of ministry (its core values) includes a preference for evangelism and growth. Though proven forms, methods, and techniques are not discarded at a whim, the church is more concerned with its outreach and effectiveness than adherence to traditions. Score 5.
- If there is only a moderate level of concern for outreach and effectiveness, score 3.
- The church's ministry forms and techniques have changed little over the years while its ministry effectiveness has diminished. Score 1.

5   3   1

4. Motivation.

- The pastor and the board have a strong sense of urgency for growth that is shared by the congregation. The congregational culture emphasizes the need for constant growth. Score 3.
- The pastor and/or the board (most of whom have been in their positions for many years) along with the congregation are bound by long-standing traditions that are growth-resistant and discourage risk taking. Score 1.
- If somewhere between these two, score 2.

3   2   1

5. Organizational Context.

- How does a growth emphasis affect the other programs in the church (Christian education, worship, missions, etc.)? If the individuals in charge are all working together for outreach and growth, score 3.
- If some are, score 2.
- If many are opposed to growth and/or are in conflict with one another over change, score 1.

3   2   1

6. Processes/Functions.

- Significant growth in a church almost always requires redesigning processes and functions in all the ministries of the church such as Christian education, church worship, etc. If most in charge of these areas are open to growth, score 3.
- If only some, score 2.

- If they are turf protectors or put their areas of ministry ahead of the church as a whole, score 1.

3   2   1

✓ 7. Ministry Awareness.

- Does the leadership of your church keep up with what is taking place in the innovative evangelical churches in the community and across America in terms of ministry and outreach effectiveness? Does it objectively compare what it is doing to that of churches that are very similar to it? If the answer is yes, score 3.
- If the answer is sometimes, score 2.
- If no comparison is done, score 1.

3   2   1

✓ 8. Community Focus.

- Does the church know and understand the people in the community—their needs, hopes, aspirations? Does it stay in direct contact with them? Does it regularly seek to reach them? If the answer is yes, score 3.
- If moderately so, score 2.
- If the church is not in touch with its community and focuses primarily on itself, score 1.

3   2   1

9. Evaluation.

- Does the church regularly evaluate its ministries? Does it evaluate its ministries in light of its vision and goals? Are these ministries regularly adjusted in response to the evaluations? If all of this takes place, score 3.
- If some evaluation takes place, score 2.
- If none, score 1.

3   2   1

10. Rewards.

- Growth is easier if the leaders and those involved in ministry are rewarded in some way for taking risks and looking for new solutions to their ministry problems. Also, rewarding ministry teams is more effective than rewarding solo performances. If this characterizes your church, score 3.

- If sometimes, score 2.
- If your church rewards the status quo and a maintenance mentality, score 1.

3   2   1

11. Organizational Structure.

- The best situation is a flexible church where change is well received and takes place periodically, not every day. If this is true of your church, score 3.
- Some churches are very rigid in their structure and either have changed very little in the last five years or have experienced several futile attempts at change to no avail, score 1.
- If somewhere between these two, score 2.

3   2   1

12. Communication.

- Does your church have a variety of means for two-way communication? Do most understand and use it, and does it reach all levels of the congregation? If so, score 3.
- If only moderately true, score 2.
- If communication is poor, primarily one-way and top-down, score 1.

3   2   1

13. Organizational Hierarchy.

- Is your church decentralized (has few if any levels of leadership between the congregation and the pastor or the board)? If so, score 3.
- If there are people on staff levels or boards/committees who come between the congregation and the pastor or the board, then more potential exists for them to block essential growth, score 1.
- If somewhere between these two, score 2.

3   2   1

14. Prior Growth.

- Churches will most readily grow if they have successfully grown in the recent past, score 3.
- If some growth, score 2.
- If no one can remember the last time the church grew, if such

growth efforts failed, or if they left people angry and resentful, score 1.

3   2   1

15. Morale.
- Do the church staff and volunteers enjoy the church and take responsibility for their ministries? Do they trust the pastor and/ or the board? If so, score 3.
- If moderately so, score 2.
- Do few people volunteer and are there signs of low team spirit? Is there mistrust between leaders and followers and between the various ministries? If so, score 1.

3   2   1

✓ 16. Innovation.
- The church tries new things. People feel free to implement new ideas on a consistent basis. People have the freedom to make choices and solve problems regarding their ministries. If this describes your church, score 3.
- If this is somewhat true, score 2.
- If ministries are ensnared in bureaucratic red tape and permission from "on high" must be obtained before anything happens, score 1.

3   2   1

✓ 17. Decision-Making.
- Does the church leadership listen carefully to a wide variety of suggestions from all the congregation? After it has gathered the appropriate information, does it make decisions quickly? If so, score 3.
- If moderately so, score 2.
- Does the leadership listen only to a select few and take forever to make a decision? Is there conflict during the process, and after a decision is made, is there confusion and turmoil? Then, score 1.

3   2   1

Total Score:_____

If Your Score Is:

47–57: The chances are good that your ministry may experience growth, especially if your scores are high on items 1–3.

28–46: Growth may take place but with varying success. Chances increase the higher the score on items 1–3. Note areas with low scores and focus on improvement before attempting change on a large scale.

17–27: Growth will not likely take place. Note areas with low scores and attempt to improve them if possible. Consider starting a new church and implement your ideas in a more growth-friendly context.

For additional copies, please write or call:

Vision Ministries International
5041 Urban Crest
Dallas, TX 75227
(214) 841-3777

Cost: $3.00/copy (includes postage and handling)

Index

Aubrey Malphurs is the president of Vision Ministries International and is available for consultation on various topics related to leadership, vision, church planting, church renewal, etc. Those wishing to contact him for consulting or speaking engagements may do so through

Vision Ministries International
5041 Urban Crest
Dallas, TX 75227
(214) 841-3777

Making Peace in the Battle of the Sexes

Randy grew up in a dysfunctional home, the son of an alcoholic father and emotionally detached mother. He struggled with feelings of not being competent, having never received emotional support and affirmation from his father.

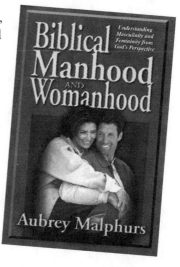

Carol grew up in a single-parent home where she decided as a young person to control her life and protect herself from emotional pain. For Carol, relationships meant danger. She wanted to avoid reliving the hurt she felt in losing her father through divorce.

Randy and Carol meet at church, become Christians, and later marry. How are they to understand the Bible's teaching on what it means to be a man and a woman related to one another as God intended?

Members of the baby boom and baby bust generations can relate to the struggles of Randy and Carol. *Biblical Manhood and Womanhood: Understanding Masculinity and Femininity from God's Perspective* by Aubrey Malphurs provides a practical and biblical guide to building marriages that reflect God's plan for personal fulfillment and marital happiness.